Howard Pyle

A Modern Aladdin

The wonderful adventures of Oliver Munier, an extravaganza in four acts

Howard Pyle

A Modern Aladdin
The wonderful adventures of Oliver Munier, an extravaganza in four acts

ISBN/EAN: 9783743338852

Manufactured in Europe, USA, Canada, Australia, Japa

Cover: Foto ©ninafisch / pixelio.de

Manufactured and distributed by brebook publishing software (www.brebook.com)

Howard Pyle

A Modern Aladdin

UNIV. OF
CALIFORNIA

A MODERN ALADDIN

OR, THE WONDERFUL ADVENTURES
OF OLIVER MUNIER

An Extravaganza in Four Acts

By HOWARD PYLE
AUTHOR OF "PEPPER AND SALT" ETC.

ILLUSTRATED

NEW YORK
HARPER & BROTHERS, FRANKLIN SQUARE
1892

ILLUSTRATIONS.

"HE SAW A DULL HEAVY SMOKE ARISE TO THE CEILING"		*Frontispiece*
"HE WAS A TALL, DARK GENTLEMAN, DRESSED IN BLACK FROM HEAD TO FOOT"	*To face page*	8
"'I AM THY UNCLE,' SAID THE STRANGE GENTLEMAN"	" "	12
"AT THAT MOMENT SHE LOOKED UP"	" "	18
"HE SUDDENLY BEGAN AN UNCOUTH, GROTESQUE DANCE"	" "	22
"HE LIGHTED A MATCH AND DROPPED IT INTO THE VASE"	" "	30
"OLIVER GAVE A PIPING CRY"	" "	36
"AT THE OPEN DOOR-WAY STOOD GASPARD AND HIS MASTER"	" "	42
"CREEPING CAUTIOUSLY FORWARD, OLIVER CAME TO THE CHIMNEY-PIECE"	" "	46
"'GOOD-DAY, MONSIEUR,' SAID A FAMILIAR VOICE"	" "	56
"THE QUESTION WAS SO SUDDEN AND SO STARTLING THAT OLIVER SANK BACK IN HIS SEAT"	" "	58
"SUCH WAS THE WORKSHOP IN WHICH THE TWO LABORED TOGETHER"	" "	70
"THEY SAW ARNOLD DE VILLENEUVE, THE GREAT MASTER, UPON THE FLOOR"	" "	74
"SHE HELD THE BOOK IN THE FLAMES WHILE TALKING, HER EYES FIXED INTENTLY UPON IT"	" "	84
"HE LEANED OVER AND LOOKED INTO HER FACE"	" "	86

"AND STRIPPED THE FALSE BODY OFF OF HIM AS YOU MIGHT STRIP OFF A MAN'S COAT"	*To face page*	94
"HE SAW WITHIN AN OVAL MIRROR SET IN A HEAVY FRAME OF COPPER"	" "	98
"THE INNKEEPER SERVED HIM IN PERSON"	" "	102
"'MAD!' SAID OLIVER, 'WHY AM I MAD?'"	" "	110
"HE IS CLAD IN A LOOSE DRESSING-ROBE OF FIGURED CLOTH, AND LIES IN BED READING HIS BOOK"	" "	114
"OLIVER SPREAD OUT THE GEMS UPON THE TABLE WITH HIS HAND"	" "	124
"ENTER OLIVER AND MADEMOISELLE CÉLESTE"	" "	130
"'DO YOU KNOW,' SAID THE MARQUIS, 'WHAT A THING IT IS THAT YOU ASK?'"	" "	136
"HE SANK ON HIS KNEES BESIDE HER"	" "	140
"SHE DREW HER DOWN UNTIL THE GIRL KNEELED UPON THE FLOOR BESIDE HER"	" "	146
"'MONSIEUR THE COUNT DE ST. GERMAINE!'"	" "	148
"THE COUNT DE ST. GERMAINE, WITHOUT REMOVING HIS EYES FROM HIS VICTIM, TOOK ANOTHER DEEP, LUXURIOUS PINCH OF SNUFF"	" "	152
"OLIVER FIXED HIS GAZE UPON THE SMOOTH, BRILLIANT SURFACE OF THE GLASS"	" "	166
"THEY BEHELD THEIR MASTER LYING UPON HIS FACE UNDER THE TABLE"	" "	176
"SUDDENLY SOME ONE TOUCHED OLIVER SLIGHTLY UPON THE SHOULDER"	" "	178
"'CÉLESTE!' BREATHED OLIVER THROUGH THE CRACK OF THE DOOR"	" "	186
"HE FOUND IN HIS CLINCHED HAND A LACE CRAVAT"	" "	194
"OVER HIS SHOULDERS HE CARRIED SOMETHING LIMP, LIKE AN EMPTY SKIN, OR A BUNDLE OF CLOTHES TIED TOGETHER"	" "	198

A MODERN ALADDIN;

OR,

THE WONDERFUL ADVENTURES OF OLIVER MUNIER.

An Extravaganza in Four Acts.

A MODERN ALADDIN.

PROLOGUE.

The Comte de St.-Germaine was a real historical character. Of all the many adventurers brilliant and volatile that flitted across the polished surface of Parisian life during the gay butterfly days of La Pompadour, none was more interesting, none left a more fascinating reflection, than he. No one knew who he was, no one knew his antecedents, no one knew whence he came, but there he suddenly appeared, to shine transiently and somewhat luridly for a year or two in a certain heaven of quasi high life.

Nothing could have been more sudden than his advent. One day he was unheard of; the next, all the world talked of him, gazed at him, and wondered. Great people adopted him and made much of him; courtiers and cabinet ministers bowed to him; the king petted him, talked with him in his privy closet by the hour, and held long and intimate discourse with him. He possessed the rare and distinguished privilege of a free and familiar entrée to Madame de Pompadour's dressing-room — a crowning honor, and one only enjoyed by the greatest and most favored courtiers.

And, indeed, the Parisian world had more cause to wonder and to marvel at him than at many another star that shone at different times in that firmament. First it was a whisper that got about that he was three, some said four, and others five hundred years old. Then it was said that there were those who had known him, gay, handsome, brilliant, fifty years before — as gay, as handsome, as brilliant. Then came a second whispering rumor—that he was the richest man in the world—a rumor also somewhat confirmed, for there were those, whose word was indisputable, who vouched to his having shown them incalculable treasures of diamonds. He himself never laid claim either to the extreme age or to the incalculable treasure, but the world claimed the one and talked of the other for him. And all the talk and gossip seemed to be built upon good foundation.

For example, said Madame de Pompadour to

him one day, "But you do not tell us your age, and yet the Comtess de Gergy, who was ambassadress at Vienna more than fifty years ago, says that she saw you there then exactly the same as you now appear."

"It is quite true, madame," replied St.-Germaine, quietly, "that I knew Madame de Gergy many years ago."

"But, according to her account, you must be more than a hundred years old?"

"That is not impossible," said he; and then added, laughing, "but it is quite possible that the countess is in her dotage."

As for his vast wealth, that also stood upon substantial foundation. The Baron de Sleichen says, in his Memoirs, that one day the count showed him so many diamonds that he thought he saw all the treasures of Aladdin's lamp spread out before him. He showed Madame de Pompadour a little box of precious stones worth more than half a million livres. Says Madame de Hausset: "The count came to see Madame de Pompadour, who was very ill. He showed her diamonds enough to furnish a king's treasury. At still another time, when a number of the principal courtiers were present, he visited madame's apartments wearing magnificent diamond knee and shoe buckles. At her request he went into an adjoining apartment and removed them for closer inspection. They were worth, M. de Gontat said, not less than twenty thousand livres."

So it came about that the Comte de St.-Germaine shone, a brilliant star in his firmament, for a while; then suddenly he vanished, and the Parisian world saw him no more. For six days that world wondered and speculated concerning his disappearance; then, on the seventh day, it forgot him.

ACT I.

SCENE FIRST.—*A street in Flourens, the house of the late Jean Munier, tailor, in the foreground.*

FLOURENS was a little town lying quite out of the usual route of young English travellers of rich connections making the "grand tour," and so, having nothing to recommend it in itself, was unknown to the great world without—dull, stupid, stagnant. Hardly ever a visitor from that great outside world appeared within the circle of its hopeless isolation. So it was a very strange thing to the town when one morning a great coach, as big as a house, dragged by four horses, with postilions clad in scarlet faced with blue, their legs incased in huge jack-boots, and each with a club queue as thick as his wrist hanging down his back, came whirling, rattling, lumbering, in the midst of a swirling cloud of dust, into the silence of the town. It was twice wonderful when the coach stopped at the inn, and it was thrice wonderful when an odd, lean, wizened little man, evidently the servant, let down the steps and helped a strange gentleman from within. He was a tall, dark gentleman, dressed in black from head to foot—from the black hat with the black feather to the black silk stockings. From the gentleman's shoulder hung a long black cloak trimmed and lined with black fur, and Flourens had never seen his like before. He neither looked to the right nor to the left, but, without saying good or bad to any living soul, he and the odd, lean little servant entered the inn, leaving the crowd that stood without staring and gaping after him. Then the great coach disappeared through the arched gate that led to the stable-yard, but it was a long time before the crowd began to disperse, before the gossiping began to cease, before the cloud of silence and dulness and stagnation settled by degrees upon the town again. Now it was maybe an hour and a half, and the last of those who had looked and wondered had gone about their business.

All is quiet, dull, heavily silent again, and in all the bald stretch of road nothing is to be seen but two women gossiping at a gate-way, and a solitary cat upon a garden wall watching two sparrows chirping and fluttering upon the eaves.

It is with this setting that the play opens, and Oliver Munier, the son of the late Jean Munier,

"HE WAS A TALL, DARK GENTLEMAN, DRESSED IN BLACK FROM HEAD TO FOOT."

is discovered leaning against the wall of the house, basking in the sun, his blouse tucked up, his hands in his pockets, and a straw in his mouth, which he now and then chews passively in drowsy laziness. Within, his mother is busied about the house-work, now and then rattling and stirring among the pots and pans, now and then scolding at him in a shrill, high-pitched voice, to which he listens with half-shut eyes, chewing his straw the while.

"I know not," said she, stopping for a moment in her work that her words might have more force in the pause—"I know not whether thou wert born so, but thou art the laziest scamp that ever my two eyes saw. Here art thou eighteen years old, and yet hast never earned a single sou to pay for keeping body and soul together since thy poor father died five months ago. Poor soul! with him it was snip, snip, snip, stitch, stitch, stitch. There was never a tailor in Picardy like him. His poor legs were bent like crooked billets from sitting cross-legged, and his poor fingers were as rough as horn from the prick of the needle. Thou lazy vagabond, with him it was work, work, work."

"Perhaps," said Oliver, without turning his head, "it was hard work that killed my poor father."

"Perhaps it was," said his mother; "but it will never do thee a harm."

Oliver shifted the straw he was chewing from one side of his mouth to the other. "Very well," said he. "Is not one in the family enough to die of the same thing?"

"Humph!" said his mother, and went back to her work with more clatter than ever.

Just then, at the farther end of the street, the inn door opened, and the strange gentleman in black came out, followed first by his servant, and then by Pierre, the landlord. He stopped for a moment at the head of a flight of stone steps, and Pierre pointed, as Oliver thought, towards their house. Then the strange gentleman came slowly down the steps, and picking his way around the puddles where the water from the trough flowed across the road and followed by his servant, came down the street towards where Oliver stood. At his coming a sudden breeze of interest seemed to awaken in the street. The two gossips turned and looked after him; the cat sat up on the wall, and also looked; and the two sparrows stopped chirping, and seemed to look. Two or three women appeared at the door-ways with children; three or four heads were thrust out at the windows, and Oliver, taking his hands out of his pockets, removed the straw that he might see better without the interruption of chewing.

The strange gentleman, when he had come to within a little distance of Oliver, stopped, and beckoning to the little lean serving-man who followed him, held a short whispered talk with him. The little lean serving-man nodded, and then the stranger came straight across the street.

Oliver gaped like a fish.

"You are Oliver Munier?" said the strange gentleman.

"Yes," said Oliver, "I am."

The strange gentleman opened his arms, and before Oliver knew what had happened, he found himself being embraced in the open street, with all those looking on.

"I am thy uncle," said the strange gentleman, with a gulp, and thereupon, releasing Oliver, he took a fine cambric handkerchief out of his pocket and wiped his eyes.

Oliver stood dumb and gaping. He did not know whether he was asleep or awake. "My uncle!" he repeated, stupidly, at last.

"Yes, thy uncle."

"My uncle!" repeated Oliver again.

"And thy dear mother?" asked the strange gentleman.

"She is in the house," said Oliver; and then he called, "Mother! mother!"

And his mother, stopping the clattering with the pots and pans, came to the door, and then, seeing a strange gentleman, stood quite still and stared.

"Mother," said Oliver, "here is a man who says he is my uncle."

"Your what?" said his mother.

"My uncle."

"Your uncle?"

"His uncle," said the strange gentleman.

"I never knew the child had one," said Oliver's mother.

"What," said the strange gentleman. "Did Jean Marie never speak of me—his brother Henri? Ah me! Well, perhaps he was ashamed of me, for I was the black-sheep of the flock. I have been to the Americas ever since I ran away from home two-and-thirty years ago, and now I have come back rich—very rich."

At the word "rich," Oliver's mother started as if she had been stung. "Oliver," she cried, "why do you stand gaping there like a stupid sot? You lazy vagabond, bring your uncle into the house! And you, Monsieur Brother, come in, come in!" And she almost dragged the strange gentleman through the door-way. "Brush your

"'I AM THY UNCLE,' SAID THE STRANGE GENTLEMAN."

uncle a chair, Oliver, brush your uncle a chair! There, Monsieur Brother, that is very good. Now will you not sit down and rest after having come all the way from the Americas?"

"My servant—" began the strange gentleman.

"We have room for him also; we have room for him as well," said Oliver's mother. "Come, Monsieur Servant. Oliver, dust him a chair also."

"Very good," said the strange gentleman; "but it is not that. I had thought that a little supper—"

"He shall have his supper," said Oliver's mother. "There is enough for him and for all the rest of us; but no thanks to that son of mine for that. As lazy a vagabond as ever you saw, Monsieur Brother. He, too, might have been a tailor, as was his father; but no, he will not work. He would rather beg or starve than work."

"That is of no importance," said the strange gentleman. "Oliver will have no need to work; we shall make a gentleman of Oliver. But I was about to say that I have ordered a little supper at the inn, and my servant will go and bring it. Go, Gaspard, and see that all is done well. In the mean time let us talk over family matters among ourselves. See, here am I, come, as I said, from the Americas, and without a soul belonging to me but my servant Gaspard. Let us, then, all live together—you, my sister, and Oliver and me and Gaspard. To-night I will sleep here in your house. To-morrow Oliver and I shall go to Paris and choose another lodging, for this is a poor place for the sister and the nephew of a rich American to live."

Oliver's mother looked around her. "Yes," said she, "that is true. It is a poor place, a very poor place."

. . . .

"Here is Gaspard with the little supper," said Oliver's new uncle.

Some one had knocked. Oliver opened the door, and Gaspard came in, followed by Jacques, the man from the inn, carrying a great basket upon his head. Oliver and his mother stared with open eyes and mouths, for they had never seen such a little supper as the ugly servant had fetched from the inn.

"Gaspard saw to the cooking," said the new uncle. "Gaspard is a famous cook, and I do not know how I could get along without him."

Oliver watched the servant furtively, and the longer he looked the more he felt something that made his skin creep. The servant was, as was said, a little thin, wiry man, and he had a lean, livid face and straight black hair that almost met the slanting eyebrows; he had a pair of little twinkling black eyes, mouse-like and cunning; he had thin, blue, grinning lips that showed every now and then beneath them a set of large white teeth; he had a long, sharp chin that stuck out like that of a punchinello; he was unpleasant to look at, but then he was a good servant— yes, he was a good servant; he might have had felt upon his feet for all the noise he made, and he spread the table with only a faint chink or tingle now and then to show that he was at work. So Oliver sat watching him from under his brows, while the new uncle talked with his mother.

At last Gaspard drew back from the table and bowed.

"Come," said the new uncle, drawing up a chair, "let us have supper."

·

SCENE SECOND.—*Midnight in Flourens; a flood of moonlight falling across the bare and naked street, mystic, colorless.*

Oliver felt himself rising like a bubble through the black waters of sleep. A noise, a shrill, penetrating noise, was ringing in his ears, and then suddenly, as the bubble breaks, he became wide-awake and sat up. At first he did not know where he was; then he remembered the strange gentleman—his new-found uncle—and knew that he was in the garret, and that the uncle was sleeping upon his (Oliver's) bed in the room below. So recollection came back to his newly awakened senses by bits and pieces, but all the while the shrill, penetrating sound rang in his ears. It was like, and yet it was unlike, the crying of a cat. It was the same high-pitched, tremulous strain, like the wailing of an impish baby; yet there was a difference—a subtle difference—between the crying of a cat and the long-drawn, quavering, unearthly sound that he heard, voiceless and inarticulate, in the silent loneliness of the midnight and the bewilderment of his new awakening—a difference that set his limbs to shaking, and sent the chills crawling up and down his back like cold fingers.

The sound that he heard neither rose nor fell, but continued to shrill on and on through the silence without, as though it would never come to an end. Then suddenly it ceased. Oliver sat in darkness upon the garret floor, with the blankets gathered about his chin, his teeth chattering and rattling and his limbs shuddering, partly through nervous, partly through actual chill. "Chicker, chicker, click!" sounded his teeth loudly in the hush of silence that followed. It seemed as though that silence was even harder to bear than the sound itself. "It was only a cat, it was only a cat," he muttered to himself. Then, "The devil! there it is again!"

Yes, that same strange noise was beginning again; at first so faint that Oliver was not sure that he heard it, then rising higher and higher and more and more keen. "It is only a cat, it is only a cat," muttered Oliver, faintly. He felt his scalp creeping.

Again the noise ceased as suddenly as before into the same death-like silence.

Some one was stirring in the room below; it was the American uncle. A great wave of relief swept over Oliver to find that another besides himself was awake. The next moment he heard the window that looked out into the street beneath softly and cautiously raised.

Near where he lay was an open unglazed window. It looked out into the moonlight just above the one that he had heard raised in the room below. A faint thrill of curiosity began to stir in the depth of the chaos of his fright. Strengthened by the companionship of wakefulness, he crept softly to the square hole and peered fearfully out.

The houses across the way stood black and

silent against the pale moonlit sky behind. The street between was bathed in the white glamour. In the middle of it and facing the house stood the motionless figure of a woman wrapped in the folds of a long black cloak. Just below Oliver was the window that he had heard softly raised a moment since, and out of it a head was looking. Oliver could only see the back of the head, but he knew very well that it was the American uncle's. He must have made some noise, for the head suddenly turned and looked up. He drew back with a keen thrill, afraid—but not knowing why he was afraid—of being seen. For a while he stood waiting and listening with bated breath and a beating heart, but all was silent below. Then again he peeped cautiously out over the window-sill; the head below was gone now, but the silent, motionless figure in the street was yet there.

At that moment she looked up, and Oliver saw her face. It was beautiful, but as livid as death; just such a face as might utter the sound that had awakened him to his blind terror. The eyes were fixed upon him, but not as though they saw him, and he leaned far out of the window, gazing fascinated. Presently the thin lips parted, he saw the white teeth glitter in the moonlight, and for the third time he heard that

"AT THAT MOMENT SHE LOOKED UP."

quavering, unearthly wail break out upon the night.

Suddenly the door of the house beneath opened noiselessly, and two figures stepped out into the pale glamour. One was the American uncle, the other was the clever servant Gaspard. The latter carried over his arm something that looked like a long black cloak. At their coming the sound instantly ceased, and the woman slowly turned her white ghostly face towards them. The American uncle strode up to her and caught her fiercely by the wrist, but she moved no more than if she had been dead. Oliver saw the American uncle stand looking this way and that, like one seeking for some escape; then he looked at Gaspard. The clever servant was mouthing and grimacing in a horrible, grotesque manner. Oliver could see him as plain as day, for the white moonlight shone full in his lean grisly face. He opened what he carried upon his arm; it was a long, black, bag-like hood.

Once again the tremulous, wailing cry cut through the night, at first faint, then rising higher and higher and clearer and clearer. Oliver saw his uncle shudder. Gaspard grinned; he crouched together, and held the black bag open in his hands. Oliver heard the American uncle utter a sharp word that he could not understand,

and saw him fling the wrist he held away from him.

What next passed happened in an instant. There was a leap, a swift, silent, horrible struggle, and the sound was stilled. Gaspard had drawn the black bag over the woman's head and shoulders. Then, without pausing an instant, he picked her up, flung her limp and helpless form over his shoulder like a sack of grain, turned, and with noiseless feet ran swiftly down the street. Oliver watched him as he ran into an inky shadow, flitted across a patch of moonlight, disappeared in a shadow again, appeared, disappeared, was gone. "My God!" he muttered to himself; "the bridge and the river are down there. Would he—"

When he looked again he saw that his uncle had gone back into the house.

For a long time the street below lay deserted in the silence of the moonlight. In the stillness Oliver could hear the far-away sound of running water and the distant barking of a dog. He leaned against the side of the window, watching with fascinated interest for the return of the serving-man. At last he thought that he saw a movement far down upon the moonlit street. It was Gaspard returning, without his burden. He appeared, disappeared, passed through the silent blocks of shadow, of moonlight, of shadow, with the same swift, noiseless steps, until he reached the road in front of the house. Then he stopped short; there was a momentary pause, and then he looked quickly and suddenly up. It was the face of a grinning devil from hell that Oliver saw.

Their glances met; Gaspard's eyes glistened in the moonlight. That meeting of glances was but for an instant. The next, Gaspard clapped his hands to the pit of his stomach, and bending over, writhed and twisted and doubled himself in a convulsion of silent, crazy laughter. After a while he straightened himself again, and as Oliver gazed, fascinated, he suddenly began an uncouth, grotesque dance. Around and around he spun, hopping and bobbing up and down; around, around, with his black shadow—pot-bellied, long-limbed, and spider-like—hopping beneath him. So hopping and bobbing, with wagging head and writhing, twisting limbs, he drew nearer and nearer to the door. Another leap, and he had hopped into the house, and the street was silent and deserted once more in the white moonlight.

For a while Oliver continued leaning out of the window, dazed, bewildered with what he had seen. Then he slowly drew his head in again, and with trembling limbs and quaking body crawled back to his blankets that lay in a heap upon the floor in the darkness. He heard a distant clock strike two; he would have given ten years of his life for a ray of good, honest sunlight.

The Morning.

"Did the cats annoy you last night?" said Oliver's mother, as they sat at breakfast.

"No," said the new uncle. Gaspard and he looked as if they had never opened their eyes the whole night through.

Oliver sat with the untasted breakfast before him, heavily burdened with the recollection of what he had seen. For one moment he woke to the question and answer, and wondered vaguely whether the little supper of the night before had given him the nightmare. Then his heart sank back, heavier than ever, for he knew that what he had seen he had seen with his waking eyes.

Suddenly the new uncle looked up. "We will start for Paris," said he, "at nine o'clock."

Oliver's heart thrilled at the words. It was on his tongue to say, "I do not want to go to Paris," but Gaspard's mouse-like eyes were fixed upon him, and he gulped, shuddered, and sat silent.

"HE SUDDENLY BEGAN AN UNCOUTH, GROTESQUE DANCE."

Scene Third.—*Paris.*

It was all like the hideous unreality of a nightmare to poor Oliver. For twelve hours they had travelled on and on and on, Oliver and those two dreadful mysterious beings, with only a brief stop now and then to change horses, and now and then for a bite to eat. At such times that one whom Oliver afterwards knew as "the master," got out and walked up and down, while the other attended to his duties as servant. But Oliver always sat still, and shrunk together in the corner of the coach, weighed down with the tremendous remembrance of what had passed the night before, and by no less looming apprehensions of what was to come. Gaspard always brought him something to eat, but he had no appetite for the food, and he shuddered at the lean, grisly face whenever it appeared at the door of the coach.

Then again the master would enter, and they would resume the never-ending journey. At last, overpowered by the continued intensity of the strain, Oliver fell into an uneasy sleep, in which all manner of ugly visions flitted through his mind. At last the sudden thunderous rumbling of the coach over stony streets aroused him again, and when he awoke it was to find himself in Paris. He unclosed his eyes and looked stonily out of the window. He had fallen asleep while the sun was still quite high in the sky; now it was night. The lights from the street lanterns flashed in at the window, traversed the gloomy interior of the coach, and then flashed out again; a perpetual glare shone from the windows of shops and stores; hundreds of people, passing and repassing, came and went; but poor Oliver, bewildered and stupefied, saw and felt all as a part of those dull, leaden dreams that had disturbed him in his sleep.

Nevertheless he noticed that as they still rumbled on and on, the lights grew less and less brilliant and frequent and that the travellers grew less and less numerous; that the streets grew crookeder and narrower, and the dark and gloomy houses upon either hand more ancient and crazy.

Suddenly, in a space of darkness, a hand was laid upon his knee, and a voice spoke his name—"Oliver!" He started wide awake, and a keen, sharp pang shot through him. Just then they again passed a lantern, and as the light traversed the interior of the great coach it flashed across the face of his companion thrust close to his own. The cloak which he had wrapped around him after nightfall had fallen away, his eyes shone with a strange light, and his lips were parted with a strange smile. "Were you frightened at what you saw last night?" he said.

Oliver felt as though a thunder-bolt had fallen. Twice or thrice he strove to speak, but his tongue clave to the roof of his mouth, and refused to utter a sound; he could only nod his head. The very worst thing that he feared had happened to him. He was so frightened that it gave him the stomachache. What was to befall him next? It was through a veil of dizzy terror that he looked into that face shut up with him in the narrow confines of the coach. All had become darkness again; but in the humming silence the eyeballs of his soul still saw that strangely smiling face as the eyes of his body had seen it when the lantern light flashed upon it. He crouched in his corner, shrunk together like a rabbit before the face of a serpent. Again there came another traversing flash of light, and then he saw that the face had widened to a grin.

"And you know that I am not your rich uncle from the Americas?"

Oliver nodded his head once more.

The other began laughing. "Come," said he; "you are frightened. But I am not so bad as you take me to be, or Gaspard either, for the matter of that, though he has strange habits. Also you saw what he did last night?"

For the third time Oliver nodded his head. His throat grew tighter and tighter, and he felt as though he would choke.

"Very well," said the other. "Then you understand that Gaspard and I are not to be trifled with. We are now at the end of our journey, and there is something that I would have you do for me. It was for that that I hunted you up at Flourens, and it was for that that I brought you here to Paris. If you do my bidding, no harm shall happen to you; if not—" The hand which rested upon Oliver's knee gripped it like the clutch of a hawk. "Do you understand?"

"Yes," croaked Oliver, finding his voice at last.

"Very good," said the other. "Now when we stop I shall get out first of all, then you, then Gaspard. He will follow close behind us, and if you make so much as one noise, one little outcry—" The speaker stopped abruptly. They were now in the black gloom of a crooked, unlighted street, with high walls beetling upon either side, but even in the blackness of the gloom Oliver could feel that the other made a motion with his hands as though drawing a sack or bag over his head, and he shrank together closer than ever.

Then suddenly the coach stopped. The next moment the door was flung open, and there stood Gaspard waiting. Oliver's companion stepped out upon the pavement. "Come," said he, and there was that in his voice that told Oliver that there was but one thing to do—to obey. The poor lad's legs and arms moved with a jerky, spasmodic movement, as though they did not belong to him, and Gaspard had to help him out of the coach, or else he would have fallen upon the pavement.

"That is good," said his travelling companion when he at last stood upon the sidewalk. "Our legs are cramped by sitting so long, but we will be better by the time we have walked a little distance;" and he slipped his hand under Oliver's arm.

Oliver groaned.

The moon had now risen, and though it did not reach the pavement, the still pallid light bathed the upper stories of the houses upon the other side of the street above the sharp black demarcation of the lower shadows. They passed two or three strange spirit-like shapes, ragged and wretched; but soon leaving even these behind, and turning down a sudden crooked way, they came to a dark, lonely, narrow court, utterly deserted, and silent as death. At the farther side of this court was a brick wall, black with moss and mildew. Upon this wall the pallid moonlight lay full and bright, showing a little arched door-way that seemed to lead through it to, perhaps, a garden upon the other side. Here they stopped, and Gaspard, stepping forward, drew from his pocket two rusty keys tied together by a piece of twisted parchment. He chose one of the keys, and thrust it into the lock of the gate. The lock was old and rusty. Gaspard twisted at the key until his bony fingers were livid, then with a grating noise the key slowly turned in the rusty lock. The gate opened —not into the garden, as Oliver had expected to see, but into the inky darkness of the passageway built into the wall.

"Come, my child," said Oliver's companion. "Come with me, and Gaspard will follow behind and close the gate."

Oliver looked about him with helplessly despairing eyes. Not a soul was in sight but the two. There was no help, no hope; there was nothing to do but to follow. He stepped into the passage-way after the other. The next moment Gaspard closed the gate, and he found himself in inky blackness.

"Take my hand and follow," said he who led; and his voice echoed and reverberated up and down the hollow darkness. Oliver reached blindly out until he touched the unseen hand.

With shuffling feet they moved slowly along the passage-way for the distance of twenty or thirty paces, the American uncle leading the way and holding Oliver by the hand, and Gaspard following so close behind them that sometimes it seemed to Oliver that he could feel the other's hot breath blowing upon his neck. Suddenly Oliver's guide stopped for a moment, and Oliver could hear him feeling with his feet upon the floor in front of him. Then again his echoing voice sounded, reverberating through the darkness. "Take care of the steps," said he, "for they are narrow and slippery."

In answer Oliver felt out instinctively with his foot. His toe touched the edge of a step, the first of a flight that led steeply downward into the darkness.

Down, down they went, Oliver in the middle and the other behind.

"We are at the bottom of the steps," said the echoing voice in front of Oliver, and the next instant he felt the startling jar of missing a step. Although the blackness was impenetrable, it seemed to Oliver that they had now reached a large room, for their footsteps echoed with a hollow sound, as though from high walls and a vaulted roof. His guide laid a hand upon his arm, and at the signal he stopped. Presently he heard Gaspard fumbling and rustling, and the next moment a shower of sparks were struck with flint and steel. As the tinder blazed under his breathing, Oliver saw that Gaspard leaned over a small brazen vase that sat upon the ground. He lighted a match and dropped it into the vase, and instantly a vivid greenish light blazed up, dancing now higher, now lower, and lighting up all the surrounding space. Then Oliver saw that he was indeed in a high, vaulted, cellar-like apartment, without window or other entrance than that through which they had come. In the centre of this vaulted space, and not far from where they stood, was a trap-door of iron, to which was attached an iron ring; a wide, heavy iron bar, fastened to the floor at one end by a hinge and at the other by a staple and padlock, crossed the iron plate, and locked it to the floor. Again Gaspard drew out the two keys, and fitting the second into the padlock, gave it a turn. The padlock gaped. He loosed it from the staple, and swung back the iron bar, creaking and grating upon its rusty hinge; then, clutching the ring in the lid of the trap, he bent his back and heaved. The iron plate swung slowly and heavily up, and as Oliver looked down, he saw a glim-

"HE LIGHTED A MATCH AND DROPPED IT INTO THE VASE."

mering flight of stone steps that led into the yawning blackness beneath.

Gaspard reached down into the square hole, and after fumbling around for a moment, drew forth an ancient rusty lantern with the end of a half-burnt candle still in it, which he proceeded to light.

Then he who was the master spoke again. "Oliver, my child," said he, smoothly, "down below there are three rooms; in the farthermost room of the three is a small stone pillar, and on it are two bottles of water. Bring them up here to me, and I will make you so rich that you shall never want for anything more in this world."

"Am I—am I to go down there alone?" said Oliver, hoarsely.

"Yes," said the other, "alone; but we, Gaspard and I, will wait here for you."

"And what then?"

"Then I will make you rich."

Oliver looked into the face of the other. In its cold depth he saw something that chilled his heart to the very centre. He turned, and, leaning forward, gazed stupidly down into the gaping hole at his feet; then he drew back. "My God!" he said, "I—cannot go—down there alone."

"But you must go," said the other.

"I—I cannot go alone," said Oliver again.

The other turned his head. "Gaspard!" said he. That was all; but the perfect servant understood. He stepped forward and laid his hand upon Oliver's wrist, and his fingers were like steel wires.

Oliver looked into his face with wide eyes. He saw there that which he had seen the night before. "I—will—go," said he, in a choking voice.

He reached out blindly a hand as cold as death, and trembling as with a palsy. One of the others, he knew not which, thrust the lantern into it. Then he turned mechanically, and, automaton-like, began descending the narrow steps. There were ten or a dozen of them, leading steeply downward, and at the bottom was a small vestibule a few feet square. Oliver looked back, and saw the two faces peering down at him through the square opening above; then he turned again. In front of him was an arched door-way like that through which he had first come. On the wall around the door-way and on the floor was painted a broad, blood-red, unbroken line, with this figure marked at intervals upon it:

☥

The door was opened a crack. Oliver reached out and pushed it, and then noiselessly, even in that dead silence, it swung slowly open upon the darkness within.

Scene Fourth.—*The three mysterious rooms.*

Oliver hesitated a moment, and then entered the cavernous blackness beyond. There he stopped again, and stood looking about him by the dusky glimmer of the lantern, which threw round swaying patches of light upon the floor and on the ceiling above, and three large squares of yellow light upon the walls around.

Oliver wondered dully whether he was in a dream, for such a place he had never beheld before in all his life. Upon the floor lay soft, heavy rugs and carpets, blackened and mildewed with age, but still showing here and there gorgeous patches of coloring. Upon the wall hung faded tapestry and silken hangings draped in dark, motionless, mysterious folds. Around stood divans and couches covered with soft and luxurious cushions embroidered with silk long since faded, and silver thread long since tarnished to an inky blackness.

In the middle of the room stood an ebony table inlaid with ivory and mother-of-pearl; above it hung a lamp inlaid with gold and swung from the arched stone ceiling above by three golden chains. Beside the table stood a chair of some dark red wood, richly inlaid like the table, with ivory and mother-of-pearl, and by the chair leaned a lute ready strung, as though just laid aside by the performer, though the strings, long untouched, were thick and fuzzy with green mildew. Upon the chair was a tasselled cushion, one time rich and ornate, now covered with great blotches of decay. Upon the table were two golden trays — one of them containing a small mass of mildew that might at one time have been fruit or confections of some sort; the other, an empty glass vase or decanter as clear as crystal, but stained with the dry dregs of wine, and two long crystal glasses, one of them overset and with the stem broken. In a dim distant corner of this one-time magnificent room stood a draped couch or bed, with heavy hangings tattered and stained with rot, the once white linen mildewed and smeared with age.

All these things Oliver saw as he stood in the door-way looking slowly and breathlessly around him; then, of a sudden, his heart tightened and shrunk together, the lantern in his hand trembled and swayed, for upon the bed, silent and motionless, he saw the dim, dark outline of a woman's figure lying still and silent.

"Who — who is there?" he quavered, tremulously; but no answering voice broke the silence.

As he stood there, with his heart beating and thumping in his throat, with beads of cold sweat standing on his forehead, and now and then swallowing at the dryness in his throat, a fragment of the hangings above the bed, loosened perhaps by the breath of air that had come in through the open door behind, broke from its rotten threads, and dropped silent and bat-like to the floor. Oliver winked rapidly in the intensity of high-keyed nervous strain. How long he stood there he could never tell, but suddenly the voice of the master breathed through the stillness behind him and from above: "Hast thou found the bottles of water?"

Oliver started, and then, with the same jerky automaton-like steps with which he had descended the stone stair-way from above, he began crossing the room to the arrased door-way which he dimly distinguished upon the other side of the apartment.

Midway he stopped, and, turning his head, looked again at the silent figure lying upon the bed. He was nearer to it now, and could see it more clearly in the dim yellow light of the lantern. The face was hidden, but the floating, wavy hair, loosened from a golden band which glimmered faintly in the raven blackness, lay spread in shadow-like masses over the stained and faded surface of the silken pillow upon which the head lay.

Impelled by a sudden impulse of a grotesque curiosity, Oliver, after a moment's hesitation, crept slowly and steathily towards that silent occupant of the silent room, holding his lantern forward at arm's-length before him.

As the advancing light crept slowly around the figure, Oliver saw first one thing and then another. First, the quaint and curious costume of a kind of which he had never seen before, woven of rich and heavy silk, and rendered still more stiff by the seed-pearls with which it was embroidered. Then the neck and breast, covered by the folds of a faded silken scarf. Then, as the light crept still farther around the figure, he saw it twinkle upon a gold and jewelled object.

Oliver knew very well what it was, and his knees smote together when he saw it. It was the haft of a dagger, and the blade was driven up to the guard into the silent bosom. He raised the lantern still farther, and the light shone full in the face. Oliver gave a piping cry, and, stumbling backward, nearly let fall the lantern upon the floor. He had seen the face of a grinning skull gazing with hollow, sightless sockets, into his own eyes.

"OLIVER GAVE A PIPING CRY."

For a while Oliver stood in the middle of the room, staring with blank, stony horror at the silent figure. Then for a second time the voice of the watcher above breathed through the silence—"Have you found the water yet?"

Oliver turned stupidly, and with dull, heavy steps passed through the door-way into the room beyond, holding the lantern before him.

Here, again, were the same rotting, mildewed richness and profusion, but they were of a different character. A long table in the centre of the room, covered with the remnant of what had once been a white linen table-cloth, and set with blackened and tarnished plates and dishes, and dust-covered goblets, and beakers of ancient cut and crystal-like glass, showed that it was a dining apartment into which he had now come. Two richly-carved chairs, with their indented cushions, were pushed back as though their occupant had but just now quitted them.

Oliver felt a wave of relief; here was no silent figure to frighten him with its ghostly, voiceless presence.

Upon the other side of this room was another tapestried door-way similiar to that through which he had just entered. Passing through it, he found himself in a low, narrow passage, barred at the farther end by a heavy iron-bound door, worm-eaten and red with the stain of rust, and with great wrought-iron hinges spreading out upon its surface like twisted fingers. Oliver pressed his foot against it. It was not locked, and it swung slowly and stiffly open with a dull groaning of the rusty hinges. Within was a stone-paved apartment, very different from those which he had just left.

All around were scattered quaint and curious jars and retorts of coarse glass and metal. Rows of bottles of different shapes and sizes stood upon the shelves, and in the corner was a great heap of mouldering, dusty books, huge of size, and fastened with metal clasps. Built into the middle of the farther wall was a wide brick chimney-place, black with ancient soot, wherein were several furnaces of different sizes, all long since cold, and with the sparks of fiery life dead in their bosoms. Nevertheless, everything had been left as though the room had been newly deserted. One pot-bellied retort reclined tipsily upon its bed of cold gray ashes; a mortar stood upon the hob of another furnace with the pestle in it; a book, held open by a glass rod across the pages, lay near by, as though for reference.

In the centre of the room stood a square pillar or table of stone, and upon it were two bottles containing a clear, limpid liquid, in appearance like distilled water. Each was stoppered with glass, and sealed besides with a great mass of blood-red wax. Upon each of the bottles was pasted a square parchment label. One was marked in red pigment, thus— ⟨symbol⟩ The other was marked thus—⟨symbol⟩ in ⟨symbol⟩ black. Oliver knew that these were the bottles for which he had been sent.

He hesitated a moment; then, reaching forth his hand, he took first one and then the other, and thrust them into his pocket.

He had reached the ending of his task.

Then of a sudden it was as though a wave of renewed life swept over him.

He thought nothing of the greater dangers that must still await him above, at the mouth of the trap, though he had there read death in the master's eyes. He was unreasonably, unthinkingly elated; it was as though he had reached the ending of a long nightmare journey, and as though his face was turned towards the light again. It was with firmer and less fearful steps that he retraced his way through the dining-room and the room beyond, where lay that silent, grisly sleeper, and so came to the door-way with the blood-red line drawn around it.

Then he stopped and looked up.

At the square mouth of the shaft he saw the

two faces still peering down at him, the face of Gaspard and the face of the master side by side.

Again, and for the third time, the master asked him the question, "Have you found the bottles of water?"

"Yes," said Oliver, "I have found them."

"Then give them to me," said the other, in a ringing voice, and he reached his arm down towards Oliver where he still stood in the door-way, around which was drawn the blood-red line.

In the reaction from the prostration of fear which had been upon Oliver for all this time, in the new elation which possessed him, it was as though he had come up from out of the dark waters which had overwhelmed him, and stood again upon the firm ground of courage.

"Yes," said he, "very good, my dear American uncle, but wait a little; what then is to come of me if I give you these two bottles of water?"

The other drew back his hand. "Did I not promise," said he, "to make you rich for as long as you lived?"

"Yes," said Oliver, "you did, but I do not believe you. Suppose that I give you these two bottles, how do I then know that you will not bang down that trap upon me, and lock me in here to die alone in a day or two?"

"Then come up here," said the other, "if you are afraid."

"Yes," said Oliver; "but last night I saw something—" He stopped short, for the recollection of it stuck in his throat. "Suppose you should hand me over to Gaspard and his black bag;" and he shuddered with a sudden creep at the thought of it.

The master's face grew as black as thunder, and his eyes shone blue in the light of the lantern. "Peste!" he cried, stamping his foot upon the stone pavement. "Do you chaffer with me? Will you give me the water, or will you not?"

"No," cried Oliver; "not until you promise to let me go safe back home."

"You will not give the bottles to me?"

"No!"

There was a pause for a moment, but only for a moment. Then there was a snarl like the snarl of a wild beast—"Gaspard!" cried the master. As he cried he leaped forward and down, two steps at a time, with the servant at his heels.

Oliver ran back into the room, yelling, stumbled over the corner of a rug, dropped the lantern, and fell flat upon the floor, where he lay, with his face buried in his hands, screaming with terror. In his ears rang a confused noise of snarls and cries and oaths and scuffling feet, but no hand was laid upon him. Moment after moment passed. Oliver raised his face from his hands, and looked fearfully over his shoulder.

At the open door-way stood Gaspard and his master, with white faces and gleaming teeth, dancing and hopping up and down, tossing their hooked, claw-like hands in the air, foaming with rage, snarling and gnashing like wolves. The lantern which Oliver had dropped still burned with a sickly, flickering gleam, for the candle had not gone out, and it was partly by the light of it that he beheld them.

Then, like a flash of lightning, he saw it all: *they could not cross that red line drawn across the door-way.*

Oliver's courage came back to him with a bound. He sat up and looked at them struggling and striving to get at him, and kept back as by an unseen wall of adamant. Instinctively he reached out and raised the overturned lantern, for the light was on the verge of flickering out.

"Promise me that I shall reach home safe and sound," said he, "and you shall yet have the two bottles."

The master did not seem to hear him. Oliver repeated the words. Then suddenly the other ceased from the violence of his gestures and exclamations, shook himself, and stood erect, pulled

"AT THE OPEN DOOR-WAY STOOD GASPARD AND HIS MASTER."

down his lace cuffs, and wiped his face with his cambric handkerchief. Then he fixed upon Oliver a basilisk glance, and smiled a dreadful smile.

"Gaspard," said he, "let us go."

He turned and walked up the stone steps again, closely followed by his servant, and poor Oliver sat staring stonily after them.

Above, the master gave an order. Oliver heard a grating, grinding noise. There was a crash that echoed clamorously through the stillness, a clanking rattle, a grating screech, a click, and then the silence of death.

Gaspard had shut and locked the trap-door above.

Oliver sat dazed and bewildered by the suddenness of what had happened. Presently he turned his head mechanically and looked around, and his eyes fell upon the silent occupant of the bed.

Then he leaped to his feet, and up the steep flight of stone steps like a madman. He dashed his fist against the cold iron lid above his head. "Open," he shouted—"open and let me out. Let me out and you shall have everything. Here are the bottles of water. Do you not want them?"

He stopped short and listened, crouching upon the upper step, close against the iron lid above him. He fancied he heard a faint sound of footsteps.

"Let me out!" he screamed again.

Nothing but dead, solemn silence.

Oliver ran down the steps again, the accursed glass bottles clicking together in his pocket. In the narrow vestibule below he stood for a moment, gazing down upon the floor in the utter abandonment of blank despair. At last he looked up, and then crawled fearfully forward into the room beyond, lit by the faint glow of the lantern. He sat him down upon the floor, and burst out crying. By-and-by a blind rage filled his heart against the cruelty of his fate and against the man who had brought it all upon him. He sprang to his feet, and began striding up and down the room, muttering to himself and shaking his head. Presently he stopped, raised his clinched fists in the air and shook them. Then he broke into a laugh. "Very well," said he; "but you have not got the bottles of water!" and he felt his pockets; they were still there.

Then, as he stood there feeling the bottles in his pocket, the last misfortune of all happened to him. There was a flare, a sputter, and then—utter darkness.

The light in the lantern had gone out.

Scene Fifth.—*The same.*

Oliver stood for a while utterly stupefied by this new blow that had fallen upon him; then, with his hands stretched out in the darkness and feeling before him with his feet, he moved blindly forward. At last he found the lantern where it stood upon the floor, and kneeling down he raised the lid and felt within. Even if he had found a candle, it would have been of no use to him, for he could not have lighted it, but nothing was there but the hot, melted grease in which the wick had expired.

Oliver sat down upon the floor and hid his face upon his knees. How long he sat there he never could tell; it might have been seconds, it might have been minutes, it might have been an hour; for, like one in a broken sleep, there was to him no measurement of time.

Suddenly a thought flashed upon him, like light in the darkness: he remembered the chimney in the room beyond. Why should he not escape in that way? At the thought a great torrent of hope swept upon him; his heart swelled as though it would burst. He rose to his feet, and feeling blindly in the blackness, came first to the table, and then to the tapestried wall beyond. Inch by inch, and foot by foot he felt his way along it, now stumbling over a cushioned couch in the darkness, and now over the edge of one of the rugs. So at last he came to the corner of the room. Thence with out-stretched fingers he felt his way along over the silent folds of the hangings until he met the emptiness of the door-way.

In the same manner he crept along the wall of the room beyond, overturning in his passage a light table laden with plates and glasses, that fell with a deafening crash and tinkle of broken glass. Oliver paused for a moment in the bewilderment of the sudden noise, and then began his slow onward way again.

Thus crawling slowly along, and guiding himself by the walls, he came out through the passage-way beyond the dining apartment, and so into the laboratory. Here he had no difficulty in finding the chimney, for the moonlight shed a faint, ghostly light down the broad flue above, glimmering in a pale flickering sheen upon the bottles and glass retorts that stood around.

Creeping cautiously forward, Oliver came to the chimney-place, climbed upon one of the furnaces, and peered upward. Not twenty feet above he could see the silvery moonlit sky. Then his heart sank within him like a plummet

"CREEPING CAUTIOUSLY FORWARD, OLIVER CAME TO THE CHIMNEY-PIECE."

of lead. For just over his head were grated bars of iron, thick and ponderous, that, crossing the chimney from side to side, were built into the solid brick and stone masonry of the flue. Oliver clambered down out of the furnace again, and sat him down upon the edge of it. There for a time he perched, staring despairingly into the darkness beyond. "What shall I do next?" he muttered to himself—"what shall I do next?"

It could serve no use for him to stay where he was, among the crucibles and retorts; he might as well go into one of the other rooms. There, at least, would be a comfortable place to rest himself, and he began to feel heavily and stupidly sleepy.

Foot by foot and step by step he felt his way back again into the farthest room. He gave no thought to that other occupant, hushed in the silent sleep of death; but flinging himself down upon the first couch that he found, gathered the musty, mildewed cushions under his head, closed his eyes, and sunk heavily into the depths of a dark, dreamless sleep.

How long Oliver Munier lay in the blankness of this heavy sleep he could never know. It must have been for a great while, as he afterwards discovered. His waking was sudden and sharp, and even before he was fairly awake he knew that he heard a sound.

He opened his eyes wide and listened. There was a soft rustling, a velvety footfall, and the sound of quick, short breathing, in the silent darkness, like that of a little child. Finally he heard a suppressed sneeze.

He sat up upon the couch, and at the noise of his movements the other sound ceased, only for the quick breathing.

"Who is there?" whispered Oliver through the darkness.

For a moment or two the silence was unbroken; then came a dull, monotonous, musical sound, somewhat like the humming of a hive of bees, but rougher and more rattling. Oliver, listening with all his soul, heard the same rustling footsteps as before, and now they were coming straight towards him. There was a moment's pause, and then something leaped upon the couch beside him.

Oliver sat as though turned to stone.

He felt a faint breath upon his hand as it rested upon the cushion at his side, and then something pressed against his wrist and his arm. It was soft, warm, furry. It was a cat.

In the gush of relief at this honest, homely animal companionship Oliver broke down from his tension of nervous strain to laughing and crying at once. Reaching out his hand, he began to stroke the creature, whereupon it bowed its back and rubbed against him in dumb response.

A sudden light flashed upon him. The cat was alive; it was good honest flesh and blood; there was nothing ghostly or demoniacal about it; where it had entered it would have to go forth again, and where it so passed to and fro there must be some means of ingress and egress. Why should he not avail himself of its aid to find his way out into the daylight again?

In a few moments he had torn the mouldy silken covers of one of the cushions into small strips, had twisted these strips into a cord, and had then tied the cord around the cat's neck. Wherever the creature went now he would follow as a blind man follows his dog. He began to whistle in the excess of his relief at the new light of hope which had dawned upon him. The sound awoke shrill echoes in the black vaulted spaces, and he stopped abruptly. "Very well," said he, half aloud. "But nevertheless, my American uncle, here is a new way out of our troubles."

By force of habit he thrust his hands into his pocket; the two bottles of water were still there.

It seemed to Oliver an age before this miraculously sent conductor, this feline saving angel, made ready to take its departure. It was hours;

but there was nothing for him to do but to wait patiently for the creature to choose its own time for leaving, for should he undertake to urge it, it might grow frightened and break away from him, and so lose him the clew of escape. Yes, there was nothing to do but to wait patiently until his guide chose to bestir itself.

Oliver was ravenously hungry, but once or twice, in spite of the gnawing of his stomach, he fell into a doze in the dead, monotonous silence of the place. Nevertheless, through all his napping, he held tight to the silken cord. It was from such a doze as this that he was awakened by feeling a twitching at the silken string, which he had wrapped around his hand for the sake of precaution. The cat was stirring.

Oliver loosened the cord so as to give the animal as much freedom as possible, and then rose to his feet. The cat, disturbed by his moving, leaped lightly to the floor. It gave a faint mew, and rubbed once or twice against his legs. Oliver waited with a beating heart. At last the cat started straight across the floor, and Oliver, holding the string, followed after it. The next minute he ran against the corner of the table, stumbled over the chair that stood beside it, overturning the mildewed lute, which fell with a hollow, musical crash.

The cat had gone under the table, and Oliver had perforce to go down upon his hands and knees and follow. When he arose again he was bewildered, and knew not where he was; he had lost his bearings in the blank darkness around him.

The cat had become alarmed, and was now struggling at the string that held it, and Oliver was afraid that it would snap the cord and get away from him. He followed more rapidly, and the next moment pitched headlong across the couch in the corner. The silent occupant rattled dryly, and Oliver heard something fall with a crash upon the floor, roll for a space, and then vibrate into silence. "Oh, *mon Dieu!*" he cried, and crossed himself. He knew very well what it was that had fallen. But the cat was now struggling furiously, and there was no time to lose in qualms. He scrambled to his feet, still holding tight to the silken cord. There was no trouble now in following the lead of the animal. The next moment his head struck with terrible force against the hard stone wall; he saw forty thousand swimming stars, and for a moment was stunned and bewildered with the force of the blow.

When his wits came back to him the cat was gone, but he still held the end of the silken cord in his hand. He stooped, and felt the direction which the cord took. It ran between two of the lighter silken hangings upon the wall. He parted them and felt within, and his hand encountered empty nothingness. He felt above, below, and on each side, and his touch met the smooth, cold stones of the wall. The open space was about two feet high and three feet wide. It was thence the cat had gone.

Oliver's only chance was to follow after; accordingly he dropped upon his knees and felt within. For a foot or more the bottom of the space ran upon a line of the floor, then it dropped suddenly and sheerly as the wall of a house. How far it was to the bottom Oliver had no means of knowing. He reached down at arm's-length, but could not touch it. He crawled out of the hole again, and then reversing himself, went in feet foremost. He dropped his legs over the edge of the open space, but still he felt nothing. Upon either side he could touch the sides of the passage with his toes; below, they touched nothing. He dropped himself lower, but still felt nothing. Lower still, and still felt nothing. He let himself go to his arm's-length, and hung there flat against the wall, and felt about with his feet, but still they touched nothing.

How far was it to the bottom of that black

passage? If he let go his hold, would he be dashed to pieces below? A great wave of fright swept over him, and he struggled vehemently to raise himself up to the edge of the hole again whence he had descended, but he was helpless, powerless. In his frantic struggles his feet clashed against the sides of the passage-way, but he could nowhere gain purchase to raise himself so much as a foot.

His struggles grew fainter and fainter, and at last he hung helplessly clinging to the edge of the hole above him with cramped and nervous fingers. A red light seemed to dance before his eyes, and he felt his strength crumbling away from him like undermined earth. He breathed a short prayer, loosed his hold—and fell about six inches to the bottom of the shaft beneath.

He crouched there for a while, weak and trembling in the reaction from his terror. At last he heaved a great sigh and wiped the beads of sweat from his forehead with his sleeve. Then, rousing himself and feeling about him, he found that the passage-way continued at right angles with the bottom of the shaft. It seemed to Oliver that he could distinguish a faint gray light in the gloom with which he was enveloped. Nor was he mistaken, for, crawling slowly and painfully forward, he found that the light grew brighter and brighter.

Presently the passage took an upward turn, and by-and-by became so steep that Oliver could hardly struggle forward. At last it again became level and easy to traverse; and still the light grew brighter and brighter.

Suddenly the passage-way became horizontal again, and Oliver stopped in his forward scrambling, and, sitting helplessly down, began crying; for there in front of him, a few yards distant, the gray light of the fading evening shone in at a square window-like hole, and into it swept the sweet fresh open air, fragrant as violets after the close, dank smell of the rooms he had left.

It was through this passage-way that the silent rooms behind must have been supplied with pure air. At last Oliver roused himself, and scrambled forward and through the hole. He found that he had come through a blank wall and upon a little brick ledge or shelf that ran along it.

Not far away sat the cat by means of whose aid he had come forth thus to freedom—the end of the silken cord was still around its neck. It was a black and white mangy-looking creature, but Oliver could have kissed it in his joy. He reached out his hand towards it and called to it, but instead of answering it leaped from the brick ledge to the pavement beneath, and the next moment had disappeared into a blind alley across the narrow court upon which Oliver had come through the hole in the wall.

Oliver sat for a moment or two upon the brick ledge, looking about him. Across the way was a high windowless wall of a house, and below that, at a considerable distance, a low building with a double row of windows extending along the length of it. Close to him was a narrow door-way—the only other opening in the wall through which he had just come. The ledge upon which he sat ended abruptly at that doorway. Above him, and at the end of the alleyway, was another blind windowless wall. All this Oliver observed as he sat upon the ledge, swinging his heels. Then he turned and dropped lightly to the pavement beneath. Something chinked in his pocket as he did so; it was the two bottles of water.

"Thank Heaven!" said Oliver, heaving a sigh. "I am safe at last."

There was a sharp click of the latch of the door near to where he stood, and then it opened. "Good-day, monsieur," said a familiar voice. "Your uncle waits supper for you." It was Gaspard, the servant, who stood in the door-way, bowing and grimacing respectfully as he held it open.

Oliver staggered back against the wall behind

him, and there leaned, sick and dizzy. Presently he groaned, sick at heart, and looked up and down the length of the narrow street, but not another soul was in sight; there was nothing for him to do but to enter the door that Gaspard held open for him.

"Straight ahead, monsieur," said Gaspard, bowing as Oliver passed him. "I will show you to your uncle, who is waiting for you." He closed the door as he spoke, and, as Oliver stood aside, he passed him with another respectful bow, and led the way down the long, gloomy passage-way, lit only by a narrow window at the farther end.

SCENE SIXTH.—*The master's house.*

At the end of the passage-way Gaspard opened another door, and then, motioning with his hand, bowed respectfully for the third time.

Oliver passed through the door-way, and it was as though he had stepped from the threshold of one world into another. Never in his life had he seen anything like that world. He turned his head this way and that, looking about him in dumb bewilderment. In confused perception he saw white and gold panels, twinkling lights, tapestried furniture, inlaid cabinets glitter-

"'GOOD-DAY, MONSIEUR,' SAID A FAMILIAR VOICE."

ing with glass and china, painted screens whereon shepherds and shepherdesses piped and danced, and white-wigged ladies and gentlemen bowed and postured. A black satin mask, a painted fan, and a slender glove lay upon the blue damask upholstery of a white and gold sofa that stood against the wall—the mask, the fan, and the glove of a fine lady. But all these things Oliver saw only in the moment of passing, for Gaspard led the way directly up the long room with a step silent as that of a cat. A heavy green silk curtain hung in the door-way. Gaspard drew it aside, and Oliver, still as in a dream, passed through and found himself in a small room crowded with rare books, porcelains, crystals, and what not.

But he had no sight for them; for in front of a glowing fire, protected by a square screen exquisitely painted, and reclining in the midst of cushions on a tapestried sofa, clad in a loose, richly-embroidered, quilted dressing-robe, his white hand holding a book, between the leaves of which his finger was thrust, his smiling face turned towards Oliver—sat the master.

As Oliver entered past the bowing Gaspard, he tossed the book aside upon the table, and sprang to his feet.

"Ah, Oliver, my dear child!" he cried. "Is it

then thou again? Embrace me!" and he took the limp Oliver into his arms. "Where hast thou been?" And he drew back and looked into Oliver's face.

"I do not know," croaked Oliver, helplessly.

"Ah! Thou hast been gone a long time. Thou art hungry?"

"I was," said Oliver, wretchedly; "but I am not hungry now."

"Nay," said the other; "thou must be hungry. See! Another little supper;" and he motioned with his hand.

Oliver had not noticed it before, but there was a table spread with a white damask cloth, and with chairs placed for two.

"Let Gaspard show you to your apartment, where you may wash and refresh yourself, and by that time the little supper will be ready."

Oliver wondered what all this meant. He could scarcely believe that the smooth-spoken master and the quiet and well-trained serving-man were the same two as those white-faced demons who had grinned and gnashed at him across the blood-red line drawn around the doorway yonder, and yet he could not doubt it.

The supper was over, and the master, with his fingers locked around his glass, leaned across the

"THE QUESTION WAS SO SUDDEN AND SO STARTLING THAT OLIVER SANK BACK IN HIS SEAT."

table towards Oliver, who, after all, had made a good meal of it.

"And those bottles of water," said he. "Did we then bring them with us from that place down yonder?" He jerked his head over his shoulder.

The question was so sudden and so startling that Oliver sank back in his seat, with all the strength gone out of his back—and he was just beginning to feel more easy. He could not speak a word in answer, but he nodded his head.

"Then give them to me," said the other, sharply. And Oliver saw the delicate pointed fingers hook in spite of themselves.

But Oliver was no longer the Oliver that had sat on the bench in front of the inn at Flourens that little while ago; he had passed through much of late, he had gained wisdom, shrewdness, cunning. Instead of helplessly handing the two phials over to the other, as he might have done a few hours before, he suddenly pushed back his chair, and rose to his feet. Not far from him was a window that looked out upon the street; he stepped quickly to it, and flung it open. "Look!" he cried, in a ringing voice. "I know you now—you and your servant. You are devils! You are stronger than I, but I have some power." He drew forth the two bottles from his pocket.

"See!" said he, "here is what you have set your soul upon, and for which you desired to kill me. Without you promise me all that I ask, I will fling them both out upon the pavement beneath. And what then? They will be broken, and the water will run down into the gutter and be gone."

There was a moment of dead silence, during which Oliver stood by the open window with the two phials in his hand, and the master sat looking smilingly at him. After a while the smile broke into a laugh.

"Come, Oliver," said he, "you have learned much since I first saw you at Flourens. You are grand in your heroics. What, then, would you have of me, that you thus threaten?"

Oliver thought for a moment. "I would have you let me go from here safe and sound," said he.

"Very good," said the other. "And what else?"

"That you promise I shall suffer no harm either from you or your servant Gaspard."

"Very good. And what else?"

"That you tell me the secret of that dreadful place where I have been."

"Very good. And what else?"

"That you show me the virtue of this water."

"Very good. And what else?"

"That you let me have half the gain that is to be had from it."

"Very good. And what else?"

Oliver thought for a moment or two. "Why this!" said he; "that you tell me why you sought me out at Flourens, and how you knew that I had escaped from that pit into which you had locked me."

"Very good. And what else?"

Oliver thought for another little while. "Nothing else," said he at last.

Once more the other laughed. "If I refuse," said he, "you throw those bottles out of the window?"

Oliver nodded.

"And you know what would then happen?"

Oliver nodded again.

"And if I promise," said he, "what then?"

"I will give to you those bottles that you seek," said Oliver.

"But what shall I promise by? My honor?"

Oliver shook his head.

The other laughed. "Do you not trust that?" said he. "No? By what, then, shall I promise?"

A sudden flash of recollection passed through Oliver's mind, a sudden inspiration came to him. "Promise by this," he cried, in a ringing voice—

and he drew the figure which he had seen depicted upon the red line around the door-way at the bottom of the stone steps—the line that had kept back Gaspard and his master like a wall of adamant. The other's face grew as black as thunder. There was a sharp click—he had crushed the glass in his hand to fragments. A drop of blood fell from his palm upon the table-cloth, but he did not seem to notice it.

"Promise by that?" said he, a little hoarsely.

"Yes," said Oliver; "by that sign."

The other swallowed as though a hard lump were in his throat. "Very well," said he; "I promise."

Oliver saw that the promise would be kept. He closed the window near to which he stood. When he turned around, the other's face was smooth and smiling again.

"And now sit down," said he, "and let us finish our little supper, then I will tell you the story of those rooms yonder, and of the dead lady whom you found there."

THE STORY OF THE MYSTERIOUS CHAMBERS.

A MONOLOGUE BY THE MASTER.

I.

The master drew his chair a little more around towards the fire, and drawing a gold toothpick from his waistcoat pocket, settled himself comfortably. "Did you ever hear," said he, "of a certain Spaniard, a very learned man, a great philosopher, and a renowned alchemist, named Raymond Lulli?"

"No," said Oliver; "I never heard tell of him."

"Or of Arnold de Villeneuve, the great French doctor, also a renowned alchemist?"

"No," said Oliver, "nor of him either."

"Well, that is not surprising; your attention has not been called to such matters, and they died more than four hundred years ago. Nevertheless, the history of the room you saw down yonder relates to them, and I am about to tell you the story of it as well as I know it.

"It was luck or chance or fate, or whatever you call it, that first turned Raymond Lulli's attention to alchemy. At the time he was studying Arabic in the mountains of Aranda, at the shrine of St. James de Castello.

"When his mistress, the beautiful Ambrosia de Compastello died, Raymond Lulli took it into his head to follow a droll fashion sometimes practised in those musty old days. He made a vow—perhaps rather hastily—to devote the rest of his life to religion; to spend it in converting Mussulmans to what was called the true faith. So, to prepare himself, he began studying Arabic in the mountains of Aranda.

"One day the Father Superior sent to him a great chest of Arabian books which had just been received at the convent. Among them was a curious little volume, square and bulky, which was not written in Arabic, but in characters of a kind which Raymond had never seen before, and which somewhat resembled Hebrew. Upon the first page of the book was a picture, and upon the last page was another. The first represented a flower with a blue stalk, red and white blossoms, and leaves of pure gold, which stood upon a mountain-top, and was bent by a gust of wind which blew from a blood-red cloud. Around the flower was a circle of open eyes. Above this circle was a naked hand holding a sword transversely by the blade. Below was a heart transfixed by what appeared to be a long pointed nail or spike. The picture upon the last page of the book represented a king with a golden sword in the act of killing a naked child, and a beautiful winged figure catching the blood in a crystal vase. At the head of the first page of the text of the book were three rubricated Arabic words. Below the last page of the text were three Hebrew words, also in rubrics. All six words had a meaning, but it is not necessary to tell you what they were or what they were intended to signify.

"Now it chanced one day that Raymond was reading a volume written by one Abou Ben Hassan, surnamed Al Sofi, or the Wise. The manuscript had been sent to him by the Father Superior in the same case with the curious little volume of which I have first spoken. This work of the learned Ben Hassan was written upon the subject of hermetic philosophy. In it was one passage upon which Raymond Lulli happened, and which altered the whole course of his life. The author was descanting upon the learning and wisdom of Hermes Trismegistus, of whom, Oliver, it is altogether likely that you never heard. The passage itself ran somewhat thus (I have often read it myself): 'Since that time, so the words ran, hath never a man lived so wise as Hermes Trismegistus, saving only the great Geber (so called by the Christians, but whom the learned among the faithful knew better as Abou Moussah Djafar), who was, indeed, the ripest apple from the flowery tree of learning. He it was who wrote that great thesis, which, did it now exist (for it is, alas! lost to the world), and did there live a being possessed with deep and sufficient knowledge to read the same, would more enrich him who could interpret it, both with knowledge and with wealth, than any one who hath ever lived since the days of King Solomon. It would, moreover, teach him a knowledge of that by means of which he might prolong his life to a thousand years, if he so chose to prolong it. For the great Geber had collected with infinite pains and ripest study the wisdom hidden in the tombs and mountains of farther Egypt, and had in his work explicated those two mysterious arcana which the wisdom of ages hath striven in vain to penetrate, to wit, the secret of life and the secret of wealth. Yea, not even the great Hermes Trismegistus himself was able to solve those two questions, which are, indeed, the fruition of all learning—the attainment of unfailing life and of infinite wealth.

"'But even were that volume, in which lieth hidden those tremendous secrets, to fall into the hands of man at this day, who at present now liveth could read or interpret it, or could understand a single one of those mysterious sentences of his wherein lieth hidden the secrets of life and wealth? For hath not the great Geber himself said, "He who would understand must first climb the mountain of difficulty, and pluck from the blue stem the red and white blossoms?" Hath not he also said, "He must, last of all, drink the blood of the infant from the crystal cup of the king and the seraphim?" And who liveth now that could understand these words, much less accomplish that task which he hath set as a bar across the path-way of knowledge—to pluck that flower and to drink that blood?'

"Such, my dear Oliver, are, as near as I can recollect, the very words of the learned Abou Ben Hassan. Conceive, if you can, their effect upon Raymond Lulli. It was as though a thunder-bolt had fallen at his feet, and as though he beheld a great truth by the flash of light that accompanied it. That volume of the wise Geber, that repository of the two great secrets of the world, had fallen into his, Raymond Lulli's, hands as though blown there by the wind of fate.

"Now, at that time the most learned man in Europe, perhaps the most learned in the world, was Arnold de Villeneuve. He was the most skilful physician and the greatest scholar of his day, and was in the very height and prime of his powers. Raymond Lulli determined to apply to him for a solution of the mysteries of the little volume, and thereupon set out at once for Paris to accomplish his purpose.

"Accordingly, one morning, as Arnold sat in his cabinet engrossed in his studies, there came a rap upon the door. It was the servant, who announced a stranger below. The doctor bade the servant show him in. It was Raymond Lulli, dusty and travel-stained.

"As soon as the servant had quitted the room, he came close to the table at which Arnold sat, and addressed him in the grandiloquent way of the day, somewhat in this fashion: 'I have come a long and weary way, I have taken a bitter and toilsome journey to seek you, and to beseech of you to give me one little measure from your great storehouse of wisdom and learning.' So saying, he thrust his hand into his bosom and brought forth the little volume, wrapped carefully in the folds of a linen cloth. He opened it, and held it before the eyes of Arnold de Villeneuve. 'Tell me, master,' said he, 'in what language and with what characters is this little volume written?'

"Arnold laughed. 'It is written in ancient Chaldee, my son,' said he. 'And have you, then, sought me out to answer you such a question as that? There are many other scholars in Europe who could have told you as much.'

"'No, master,' said Raymond; 'it was not alone for that that I sought you, for, as you say, there are others that could have told me as much; but who save you could unfold to me the meaning of this?' And he opened the book at the first picture representing the flower upon the mountain-top. 'And who but you, the great Arnold de Villeneuve, could teach me how to climb the mountain of knowledge and pluck the flower of wisdom? Will you teach me that, master?'

"Arnold de Villeneuve said nothing at all, but his face had grown all at once very white. By-and-by he drew a deep breath. 'I will try to teach you the secrets of that book,' said he, after a while; 'but it will be a long and weary task, for I have first to learn very much myself.'

II.

"That morning at dinner—for they used in those days, Oliver, to dine at ten or eleven o'clock in the morning—Raymond Lulli saw for the first time Agnes de Villeneuve, who was then reputed the most beautiful woman in Paris. It was no wonder that, fresh from the ennui of the solitude of the mountains of Aranda, he should have fallen passionately in love with her. Neither was it strange that Agnes should love him. For this propinquity, Oliver, is a droll affair. It will cause a woman to fall in love with a ghoul, not to speak of one so tall and handsome as Raymond Lulli. So she loved him as passionately as he loved her. It was as natural as for steel and loadstone to come together.

"In the days and weeks that followed, Arnold de Villeneuve saw nothing of what was passing between the two. In his eyes Raymond Lulli was but a fellow-student. It did not occur to him that passion might find place even in the bosom of such an ardent follower of alchemy as this new scholar of his. He beheld only the philosopher and student; he forgot the man. For months the two labored and toiled like slaves, striving to discover those two secrets contained in the great Geber's book, and hidden beneath the strange formulas, the obscure words, and the mystic pictures. One day they seemed upon the very edge of success, the next day they failed, and had to begin again from the very beginning. The laboratory in which they conducted their great work was one in which Arnold de Villeneuve had already carried forward and completed some of his most secret, delicate, and suc-

"SUCH WAS THE WORKSHOP IN WHICH THE TWO LABORED TOGETHER."

cessful operations. Within the wall of the garden back of his house he had had a hollow passage-way constructed, which ran for some little distance to the deep cellar-like vault that had, perhaps, at one time been the dungeon of some ancient fortress. Beneath this vault or dungeon were three rooms, opening one into another, that had in a far distant period been hewn out of the solid rock. They were the rooms from which you, Oliver, escaped only a little while ago. Two of those rooms were sumptuously and luxuriously furnished; the furthermost was the laboratory where the two great problems were solved—the problem of life and the problem of wealth. Such was the workshop in which the two labored together, occasionally for days at a time; the one sometimes sleeping while the other compounded new formulas or watched the progress of slow emulsions.

"It was, as Arnold de Villeneuve had predicted, a long and toilsome labor which they had undertaken; it was, as the great Geber had said, a tremendous task to climb the steep mountain of knowledge and to pluck the mystic flower of wisdom from the top. But at last the summit was reached. Suddenly, one morning, unexpected success fell upon them like a flash of lightning; for this, like many other successes, happened through an accident—the overturning of a phial (the contents of which it had taken months to prepare) into a mortar in which Raymond was mixing a powder. It all happened in a moment—the accidental brushing of a sleeve—but that one moment was sufficient; the secret of life was discovered. From the secret of life to the secret of wealth was but a step; the one hung upon the other. The very next day they discovered that which shall make us—you, Oliver, and me, whom you may henceforth call 'master'—the richest men in France. Did you know that the diamond and the charcoal are the one and the same thing?"

"No," said Oliver, "I did not; the one is black and the other is white.

Oliver's companion laughed. "There is less difference between black and white, Oliver, and between the charcoal and the diamond, than most people think. Later you will learn that for yourself; just now you must take my word for it. But to resume our narrative. The next morning Raymond and his master, as I have said, produced from the first formula a second, by means of one drop of which they created in a closed crucible, in which five pounds of charcoal had been volatilized, a half-score of diamond crystals of various sizes, and one fine blue-white crystal of nearly eight carats in size. Oliver," cried the speaker, rising in his enthusiasm, and striding up and down the room, "that was, to my belief, the greatest discovery that the world ever saw! Other philosophers have approached the solution of the problem of life, and have prolonged their existence ten, twenty, yes, fifty years; still other philosophers have transmuted the baser metals into gold; but who ever heard of transmuting black charcoal into brilliant diamonds?" He stopped abruptly and turned towards the lad, and Oliver saw the eyes which looked into his blaze with excitement, like the diamonds of which he spoke. "Do you wonder," he cried, "that Raymond Lulli and his master acted like madmen when they opened that retort, and found those sparkling crystals twinkling like stars upon the rough surface of the metal? Ha!"

III.

"But, as I said, it was a long time before those experiments were concluded — before the great problems of life and wealth were solved. Nine months had passed since Raymond had come, dusty and travel-stained, like a beggar to the master's door, asking for crumbs of knowledge. It was the consummation of their life's success.

The very next morning after that consummation came ruin. A blow, sharp and terrible, fell upon the house.

"It was late, and the master had not yet made his appearance. Raymond Lulli, passing along the hall-way with a book under his arm, met Agnes at a door-way.

"'My father,' said she, 'has not yet come down from his room.'

"'I will call him, Agnes,' said Raymond, and then she noticed that his face was as pale as ashes.

"'Are you ill, Raymond?' she asked.

"'No—yes, I am ill,' he shuddered. 'I will go and call your father.' And he turned away.

"Agnes stood watching him as he, with slow, heavy steps, climbed the steep stairs that led to the master's room above. She watched him as he reached the door and knocked; and then, after a pause, knocked again, and then again; she watched him as he laid his hand hesitatingly upon the latch, and then raised it, and pushed open the door.

"The next moment the heavy book slipped from under his arm, and fell with a crash to the floor. 'Agnes!' he cried, 'your father!' And then his voice rang through the house: 'Jean! Franquois! Joseph! The master, help!—the master!'

"THEY SAW ARNOLD DE VILLENEUVE, THE GREAT MASTER, UPON THE FLOOR."

"There was a shriek; it was Agnes; there was a confusion of voices and of running feet, and when the people of the house crowded into and around the door-way, they saw Arnold de Villeneuve, the great master, lying upon the floor, his eyes closed, and his head resting upon his daughter's lap, as she kneeled beside him. His face was white and drawn, and every now and then he shook with a hiccough. It was not a pleasant sight, Oliver, and there was no need to ask the question—the awful gray veil of death rested upon the great doctor's face.

"At a little distance from the father and the daughter stood Raymond Lulli, with a face almost as ashen white as that of the dying man. He turned to the frightened servants.

"'Why do you stand there like fools?' he cried. 'Come, lift the master upon his bed.'

"They approached at Raymond's bidding, and, raising the dying physician, laid him back upon the bed, from which he had apparently just risen when the stroke of death fell upon him.

"Minute after minute passed in dead silence, broken only now and then by a suppressed sob from one of the servants who stood around. Agnes sat upon the bedside, silently holding her dying father's hand in hers. Half an hour went by—an hour—the end was very near. Then suddenly Arnold opened his eyes; they were sightless to this world; they were gazing straight into the shadow of eternity that hung like a curtain before him. His lips moved, and at last a struggling sound passed them.

"'Agnes!' said he, in a thick, guttural voice. 'Agnes!'

"'Here I am, father,' said she, and she leaned forward, bringing her face before his eyes; a gleam of intelligence flickered faintly in them. He beckoned stiffly, and Agnes drew still nearer. The dying man raised his hand and touched her face; he felt blindly for a moment, passing his cold, leaden fingers over her brows, and at last, as though finding her eyes, pressed his palm upon them. He held his hand there for a few seconds, and then let it fall heavily beside him, and those who looked saw Agnes's eyes were now closed. For a moment or two there was a pause of dead silence.

"It was Arnold's voice, thick, guttural, inarticulate, that broke the hush: 'Look!'

"Agnes opened her eyes.

"Arnold raised his hand, and with his forefinger began feebly drawing strange figures in the air; at first stiffly, then gradually more freely as he gathered his dying powers into one last effort.

"At first Agnes gazed at the slow-moving hand intently, wonderingly. Raymond sat near by, with his chin resting upon his palm and his eyes fixed upon the floor, brooding darkly. By-and-by those who watched saw the color fade slowly out of her cheeks; they saw her face grow pinched and her eyes dilate. At last she reached out her hand and laid it upon her father's, holding it fast in spite of his stiff and feeble efforts to release it.

"'Stop, father!' she cried. 'Oh, God! Stop, I can bear no more.'

"'Look,' said Arnold, thickly.

"He had released his hand, and now again began drawing figures in the air. All were looking at him wonderingly, excepting Raymond Lulli, who never once raised his eyes, fixed broodingly upon the floor. At last the motions ceased, and the hand fell heavily upon the bed beside the dying man. Agnes sat silent, looking into his face with a face as white. At last she spoke, in an unsteady, constrained voice.

"'Father,' said she, 'is there nothing else? Must I do that?'

"No answer.

"'Father,' said she again, 'must I do that?'

"Agnes waited for a little while, then again said:

"'Father, must I do that? Is there nothing else? Must I do that?'

"'Yes.'

"There was another space of breathless silence, and then one of the women began to cry; the others joined in with her. Arnold de Villeneuve was dead.

"Agnes arose from the side of the bed where she sat, and, without saying a word, walked slowly and stiffly out of the room.

"That same afternoon her waiting-woman came to Raymond Lulli, and told him that her mistress wished to speak with him. He followed the woman up the long flight of steps to the door of Agnes's chamber. He knocked, and heard a faint voice within bid him enter. Agnes was standing in the centre of the room, clad in a dark rich dress, heavily embroidered with seed-pearls. Her dark hair was gathered loosely behind by a golden serpent which held the locks together. There were no signs of tears upon her pale face, but her eyes were encircled by dark rings.

"Raymond stood for a moment looking at her. 'Agnes!' he cried, and then came forward into the room, and took her into his arms. She neither yielded nor resisted, but stood passive and motionless. There was something about her that struck a chill through him; he drew back, and looked into her face. 'Agnes,' he said, 'what is it? Are you ill? Do you not love me?'

"There was a moment's pause. 'Yes,' said Agnes, 'I love you.'

"Again Raymond took her in his arms, but still there was no response.

"Suddenly she laid her hand upon his breast, and drew a little back. 'Tell me,' said she—'tell me, Raymond, is there in this house a little crystal globe in a silver box?'

"Raymond hesitated. 'Yes,' said he.

"Agnes's lips moved as though she said something to herself. Then she spoke again: 'And tell me one thing more, did not you and my father discover a clear liquor by means of which you could become richer than any one in France or in the world?'

"'Yes,' said Raymond. Again he saw Agnes's lips move.

"'And tell me,' said she; 'have you not a book written in strange characters, and illuminated with two strange pictures?'

"'Yes,' said Raymond.

"Again, for the third time, Agnes moved her lips, and this time Raymond heard the words which she whispered to herself: 'Then it is true.'

"'What is true, Agnes?' said he.

"She did not seem to hear his question. 'Tell me this, Raymond,' said she, 'did not you and my father work together in a dark vaulted place under the ground?'

"'Yes,' said Raymond.

"Agnes paused for an instant. 'Then take me there, Raymond,' said she.

"For a moment or two Raymond could not speak for surprise. 'What?' he cried. 'Take you there? Take you there now, at this time?'

"'Yes, now.'

"'Agnes, I do not understand.'

"'It is of no importance that you should understand,' said she; 'only I have something to show you there that you have not yet seen, and of which you know nothing.'

"You know the path they took, Oliver; you yourself walked along it at my heels the other day. Agnes and Raymond traversed that same passage, descended the same stair that you descended, entered the vault that you entered. There Raymond Lulli unlocked the padlock and raised the trap-door as you saw Gaspard unlock the one and raise the other. He took the same lantern from the shelf within as Gaspard took it, and lit the candle as Gaspard lit it, then descending the stairs, they entered the first of the three rooms below.

"Raymond lit the lamp that you found hanging there from the ceiling, and Agnes stood for a moment looking around her. The tapestries and hangings and all that you saw were fresh and beautiful then.

"They entered the room beyond where were the remains of the supper that Raymond and his master had eaten the night before; the chairs by the table pushed carelessly back as they had left them, and as you, Oliver, found them.

"Thence they passed through the narrow passage, and entered the laboratory beyond, where Agnes saw the two sealed phials standing upon the stone table as you saw them.

"Agnes pointed with her finger towards them. 'And that,' said she—'that, then, is the precious liquor of wealth that you and my father discovered?'

"'Yes,' said Raymond.

"'And it can transmute charcoal to diamonds?'

"Raymond hesitated. 'Yes,' said he.

"Agnes turned suddenly upon him. 'And tell me, Raymond,' she said, 'have you not that little crystal globe in the silver casket?' Raymond instinctively raised his hand to his breast. 'I see you have,' said she, smiling. 'It contains the secret of life?'

"Raymond nodded his head.

"There was a pause; then Raymond said, in a hoarse voice, 'Why do you question me thus, Agnes? Do you not love me?'

"Agnes looked upon him with the same strange smile that her lips had worn ever since she had begun questioning him. 'Poor Raymond,' said she, 'do you, then, doubt my love? But tell me, have you not with you that book of knowledge, of which I spoke to you, containing the strange pictures?'

"'Yes.'

"'Let me see it;' and she held out her hand.

"Raymond hesitated. Agnes fixed her beautiful eyes upon him. 'Do you not love me, then?' said she.

"Raymond thrust his hand into his bosom, and drew from the pocket of an inner vest the little volume.

"Agnes took it, and look curiously at it. 'Raymond,' said she, 'will you give me this book for my own, to do as I choose with it?'

"Raymond made no answer.

"'You will not? Do you, then, love it more than me?' She stood holding the book, waiting for his reply.

"'I give it to you, Agnes,' said he at last.

"'And it is now mine to do with as I choose?'

"'It is yours.'

"'Give me the lantern.'

"Raymond reached it to her wonderingly. She took it, raised the slide, opened the book, and held the parchment leaves over the flame within. Raymond gave a sharp cry, 'Agnes!' He would have snatched it from her, but she laid her hand upon his arm.

"'Stop!' said she. 'Have you not all that man can desire in this world without this book? You have given it to me; it is mine, and I shall do as I choose with it. You cannot love it with all your heart and me also. Which do you choose?'

"She had held the book to the flames while talking, her eyes fixed intently upon it as the parchment leaves blackened and curled and wrinkled. Raymond groaned and turned away. The oppressive odor of the burning skin filled the air, and when Agnes cast the remains of the volume into the pit beneath the grate of the furnace, the wisdom of the great Geber, the learning that had taken him a lifetime to accumulate, was nothing but a blackened mass of stinking cinders.

"'Come,' said Agnes, 'let us leave this dark and dismal place, and go back yonder into the other room.' She led the way into the first apartment, and there sat down upon the couch, motioning Raymond to a seat beside her. 'Are you happy, Raymond?' said she.

"'Yes,' he whispered. He would have taken her into his arms, but she held up her hand.

"'Wait,' said she. 'Have you, then, all that you desire?'

"'Yes,' he said, in a trembling voice; 'with your love.'

"'Poor Raymond!'

"There was a little space of silence. And then at last she turned to him with that same strange smile upon her face. 'Do you know what my father did when he moved his hands as he did when you saw him?' said she.

"'No,' said Raymond.

"'He drew strange pictures before my eyes, Raymond, and I saw them as plainly as I see you now. Would you like me to tell you what they were?'

"Raymond nodded his head.

"'Then I shall tell you. I saw you and my father in this place together, and you had completed the last of your great experiments, and had sealed those two phials as I saw them yonder. I saw you and my father quit this place filled with joy that the last touch of your work was done. After that came the dark blank of night and of sleep. The next picture he drew was of the morning—of this morning when he died— and I saw him sleeping upon his bed. The door

"SHE HELD THE BOOK IN THE FLAMES WHILE TALKING, HER EYES FIXED INTENTLY UPON IT."

opened, and I saw you come softly in and forward to his bedside, and stand looking down at him as he slept. Above his face you drew strange characters with your finger; they were spells that he himself had taught you. After that I saw you, Raymond, draw a bunch of keys from beneath his pillow. Then I saw you go to the great iron-bound chest that stood in the corner. From within you took a little silver box; you did not open the lid, but I saw that within it was a crystal globe about as large as a dove's egg. I saw you relock the chest and replace the keys beneath my father's pillow.' Agnes was looking into Raymond's face as she spoke, and her lips still wore that same faint smile. 'What next I saw, Raymond, was this,' said she. 'You took from your pouch a little wooden box filled with a bright green powder; then from the same pouch you drew a long slender needle. Upon the point of the needle you took a little of the green powder. (All this my father drew with his dying hand in the air, Raymond.) I saw you stoop over him and thrust that long shining needle deep into his shoulder. Then you turned and left the room; but as you left it, I saw your face as I see it now, and it was as white as ashes, as it is now, and the sweat stood in beads upon your forehead, as it stands there now. What did it mean, Raymond?' Her lips never lost that strange, odd smile.

"'God, I do not know!' cried Raymond, hoarsely.

"'It meant that you murdered my father, Raymond—that you murdered the man who taught you all that you now know—that you murdered the man who in nine months made of you, a raw student, the most learned alchemist, but one, in Europe.'

"There was a long pause of dead silence. 'Agnes,' cried Raymond, in that same hoarse, dry voice, ' Agnes—I love you!'

"The smile never left her lips. 'Very good,' said she; 'but stay, I have not yet done. All that my father had showed me so far was past and gone; now he showed me what was to come. I saw us both pass through that long, dark, narrow way; I saw the dark, vaulted cellar above us; I saw us descend and stand together in the farther room yonder and look upon those phials; I saw myself burning that accursed book by the light of the candle in the lantern; I saw us seated together upon this couch as we are now. What next do you think I saw, Raymond?'

"'I do not know.'

"'I saw this!'

"There was a movement as quick as lightning,

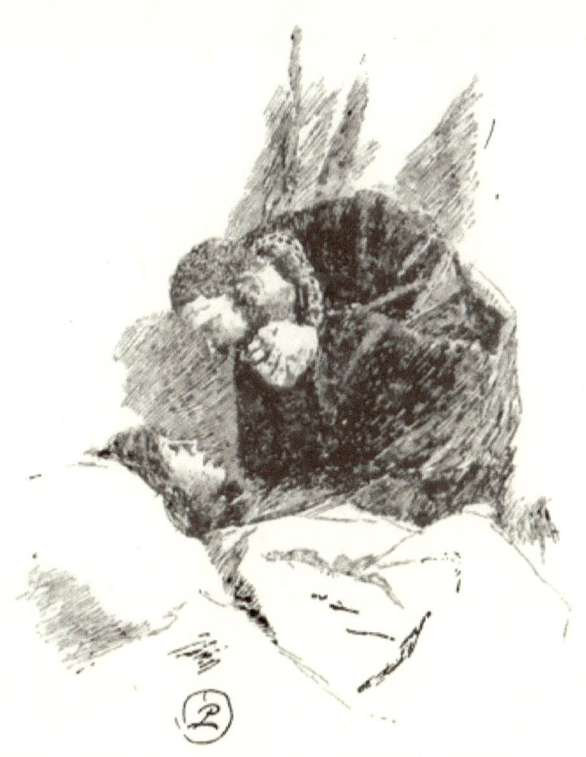

"HE LEANED OVER AND LOOKED INTO HER FACE."

a flash, a blow, a deep sigh. Agnes sat for a moment with the smile still resting upon her white lips, and something bright glistening upon her bosom. It was the handle of a dagger, and she had stabbed herself. Then she lay slowly down upon the pillow beside her.

"For one moment Raymond sat as motionless as stone; then he started up with a shrill cry. He leaned over and looked into her face; that smile was still upon her white lips.

"'Agnes!' he cried; then again, 'Agnes!' But the smiling lips never answered; she was dead.

"Raymond slowly turned, and walked heavily and stupidly out of the place, closing the door behind him. At the head of the shaft he mechanically opened the slide of the lantern, and blew out the half-burned candle, and then set the lantern upon the shelf within, as he had been used to do. He closed the trap, and lowered the bar, and snapped the padlock in the staple; then, again, with the same slow, heavy tread, he left the vaulted room, ascended the stone steps, and threaded the passage-way. He did not go back into the master's house, but passed out at the arched gate-way where we, Oliver, entered. Before he went out into the street beyond he laid his hand upon his breast to make sure the silver box containing the talisman was there; it was all that he had saved from his ruin."

IV.

"From that time Raymond Lulli led a wandering, irregular, eventful life. Under the spur of his remorse he went first to Rome and then to Tunis, where, until his life was threatened on account of his efforts to convert the Mussulmans, he devoted himself partly to the fulfilment of his original vow, partly to the further study of alchemy. After that he lived for a while in Milan; after that he went to England, where, as I have heard, he transmuted lead and quicksilver into gold to the amount of six millions rose nobles; after that he returned again to Rome; and after that for a second time to Africa, where he took up his abode at Bona.

"Now there was at that time at Bona a famous and learned professor, who had devoted himself more particularly to the study of demonology. It is hardly likely that you have ever heard his name; it was Yusef Ben Djani. I know of nobody since his time who approached him in his knowledge of the science unless, perhaps, it was the great Cornelius Agrippa.

"This learned scholar held that the power of man's will was such that, under certain circumstances, it could be so far impressed upon those diffused forces of life about us as to materialize or concentrate them, and so render them cognizant to the human understanding, or, in other words, visible. Now, Oliver, it is very well known that one man may so impress his will upon another as to render that other will entirely subservient to his own. Under such conditions, the one so impressed sees, feels, smells, tastes, and senses only as the superior will orders; he moves, speaks, and exists as the other commands. If that power, Yusef Ben Djani argued, could impress material men in this world, why could it not impress men in the world immediately beyond? Is not a man, he reasoned, the same man after quitting this world as when he lived in the body? Why, then, is he not as subject to that psychological power there as here, and why, then, could he not be influenced there as well as here? Such an influence Yusef Ben Djani did exert, and succeeded. He materialized those quiescent forces of life, and brought them into such communion with himself that he was able to compel them to that certain exudation of life in quiescence which we in this world call matter. Do you understand me, Oliver?"

Oliver shook his head. "No," said he, "I do not." He had tried to follow the other so far as he was able, but he had long gotten beyond the power of comprehension; the words fell upon his ears one after the other like blows, until his head hummed like a beehive.

The other laughed. "Very well," said he. "It is of no importance that you should comprehend Yusef Ben Djani's theory. But this at least you can understand: he materialized evil spirits.

"Now there was a certain young Venetian student named Nicholas Jovus, who almost from his chilhood had possessed a wonderful psychological power upon others. By psychological power I mean the power of superinducing his own will upon the will of another; in other words, to make such another do absolutely as he chose.

"The fame of Yusef Ben Djani was at its height, and Nicholas Jovus, then about four-and-twenty years of age, determined to visit the great master at Bona. The philosopher saw in the young student the material for an even greater than himself. He persuaded him to stay in Bona, and to study the science of demonology under him. It was while there that, with the assistance of his master, Nicholas Jovus superinduced his own will upon the surface of a mirror to such an extent that within it he could at any time see that which he willed to see. It was by means of this mirror that he one time beheld Raymond Lulli, of whom he had often heard, and, circumstances being then peculiarly propitious, beheld at the same time not only Raymond Lulli himself, but the secret of the talisman that he carried in his bosom. And not only did he discover the existence of the talisman, but (Raymond's mind being at that moment concentrated upon the past) he discovered the story of the philosopher's life as I have told it to you, and thus first gained knowledge of those dark chambers below the vault. Yes, Nicholas Jovus saw all this in the mirror just as I have described it to you, Oliver; it was the first and only time, but he never forgot it.

"Now soon after Raymond Lulli had reached Rome, after having left Paris, he was taken with a violent fever, from which he wakened, his physicians told him, only to die. But the physicians were mistaken. The next morning when they visited him he was sitting at the table eating a boiled capon, as well a man as you or I. I need to hardly tell you he had used the talisman of life.

"Yet it was only with great hesitation, and

in the last extremity, that Lulli thus rehabilitated himself with a new body, for by so doing he cut himself off forever from all chance of entering those secret chambers again and recovering the phials, which he now bitterly regretted having left behind him in the first throes of his grief and remorse. For Arnold de Villeneuve, for protection against evil powers, had drawn around the door of those underground chambers a circle upon which he had marked a sign that Raymond Lulli could not pass without leaving his newly-acquired body behind him.

"From the time that Raymond Lulli had used the talisman of life to the time that Nicholas Jovus saw him in the mirror, thirty years had elapsed, and yet he appeared as young as upon the day when the Roman physicians had told him that he was to die.

"Nicholas Jovus determined to gain that talisman for his own.

"Now the young Venetian student had a curious, odd servant, very much attached to him, and not so wicked as one might have thought under the circumstances. Early one morning, before the town was awake, Nicholas Jovus, followed by this servant, left the house of his master and hurried down to the sea-shore. He had looked in his glass and saw that Raymond Lulli was walking there. He met the alchemist not far from where a long quay ran out into the water.

"Since the time when he had first seen Raymond Lulli in the glass, Nicholas Jovus had made the acquaintance of the master in his own proper person. Accordingly, Raymond stopped and chatted awhile with the young student. While the two stood talking together that odd servant of whom I spoke stepped around behind the philosopher. He made a silent motion of inquiry, Nicholas Jovus nodded in reply, and the next moment all was over. The serving-man had — had drawn a bag over the philosopher's head.

"Nicholas Jovus thrust his hand into the philosopher's bosom, and, after feeling for a moment, found the talisman, which was enclosed in a bag hung around his neck. He did not take time to unfasten the cord from which it hung, but, giving it a jerk, broke the string with a snap.

"As he did so, Raymond Lulli, who had been lying silent in the encircling arms of that strange servant, gave a sharp, a loud, and a bitter cry.

"What followed was as unlooked-for to Nicholas Jovus as it would have been to you had you been there, Oliver. That quaint servant of his—

what think you he did? He laid Raymond Lulli upon the sand of the sea-shore, and stripped the false body off of him as you might strip off a man's coat. The young student did not know how it was done, but done it was, and as deftly and as cunningly as a fisherman might draw the skin from an eel. Then, as Nicholas Jovus stood aghast watching him, he shouldered what appeared to be the empty skin of Raymond Lulli, turned, and running some distance out along the quay, flung his burden with a splash into the water. It sunk like a stone. The Raymond Lulli that was left behind was an old man of seventy-five years of age, bruised, bleeding, dying. My faith, Oliver! It was a long time before Nicholas Jovus could bear the presence of that odd servant of his without a shudder.

"That is all concerning the story of Raymond Lulli and those rooms that you were in not long ago."

THE END OF THE MASTER'S MONOLOGUE.

He finished speaking, and Oliver sat gazing at him open-mouthed. He was bewildered—he was stunned. It began to dawn upon his stupefied wits that he was in the very presence of and

"AND STRIPPED THE FALSE BODY OFF OF HIM AS YOU MIGHT STRIP OFF A MAN'S COAT."

face to face with a dreadful, grotesque miracle. "And you," said he, in a low voice, and then stopped short, for the question stuck in his throat.

The other smiled. "And I?" said he. "What is it, then, that you would ask?"

"Are—are you—are you—Nicholas Jovus?"

The other laughed. "What a droll question!" said he. "That thing happened four hundred years ago."

Oliver's skin began to creep; but then he was growing used to that feeling. The two sat watching one another for a little while in silence, the one with dull bewilderment of wonder, the other smiling oddly. Presently the smile broke into a laugh. "You are very droll, Oliver," said he; "you would believe anything that I told you. I have seen and done many strange things in my days, but as for being four hundred years old— Bah! my child, why all this that I have been telling you is only a story, a legend, a tradition, handed down from one to another of us who dabble in alchemy; for I confess to being one of such. No doubt it has grown absurdly as it has been transmitted from man to man. Nevertheless, there are in that story some strange matters—one might almost call them coincidences—that appear to fit in with things that you have seen, and which might, with an irrational mind such as yours, strengthen absurd speculations." He sat watching Oliver smilingly for a while. "That mirror of Nicholas Jovus's," said he, suddenly — "what would you say if I had it in my own possession? Nay, what would you say if it were in this very room?" Oliver looked sharply around, and again the other laughed. "You need not be alarmed," said he; "it is very harmless. But come, I will be perfectly frank; it *is* in this room, and I will show it to you. It is my intention that we shall thoroughly understand one another, and we must arrive at such understanding now. So understanding one another, we can best be of benefit to each other. But first of all, since we are in the way of being frank, I will begin by making a confession. I confess to you, my dear child —yes, I confess frankly that the ugly suspicions that you have entertained about me have not been entirely without ground. I confess that I had not intended that you should have left that place down yonder, from which you so miraculously escaped. Perhaps this confession may at first shock you, but I am sure, when I explain matters, you will understand that I was not entirely unjustified in seeking to destroy you. I have, I think I may say, very considerable skill in foretelling events by the stars—not foretelling them perfectly, of course, for the science of astrology is not yet perfected, but looking into futurity in a general way. Nevertheless, imperfect as the science of astrology is, my reading of fate was clear enough to teach me who and what you were, and, in a general way, where you were to be found. That reading told me that, unless some heroic remedy were devised, the time drew near when you would be my ruin—" he stopped suddenly, his gaze fixed itself absently above Oliver's head, and Oliver saw his face grow pale and haggard, as if it saw some dreadful vision; he drew in his breath between his shut teeth—"and my death," said he, in a low voice, completing his speech, and shuddering as he spoke the words. Then he passed his hand over his face, and when he drew it away again his expression was as smiling and as debonair as ever. "But we will not speak of such unpleasant things," said he. "I have only mentioned them so far that you might see that I was not altogether inexcusable in seeking to rid myself of you. In conclusion. I will say that about the time that I located with some accuracy the particular spot where you were living, I also discovered that for which I had been seeking for many years—the underground cell in which was Arnold de Villeneuve's laboratory.

This house is built upon the ground whereon his stood. It is a wretched tumble-down affair, mean and squalid, yet I have fitted it up for my home; for, as you have discovered, it connects almost directly with that underground vault where the student and the master discovered their great secret.

"Unfortunately, for certain reasons that I need not mention, I could not pass that circle and the sign upon the wall around the door-way. So, not being able to pass it myself, it was a great temptation for me to send you to get those bottles for me, and then, in your destruction, to seal my own security. It was a great temptation, I say, and I yielded to it. What I did was unpleasant to you, perhaps, but that now is all passed and gone. Let it be forgotten, and hereafter we shall, I know, be great friends. That attempt has taught me a lesson. I tried, in spite of fate, to destroy you, and failed; now I will try kindness, and see if that will eliminate you from my life. I have it in my power to make you the richest man in the world—next to myself; and what is more, I will do so, and then we shall separate forever. As for me, I shall live in Paris, for there is no other place in the world for a man of parts like myself. You, upon your part, may live wherever you choose—except

"HE SAW WITHIN AN OVAL MIRROR SET IN A HEAVY FRAME OF COPPER."

in Paris. You shall quit Paris *forever*. Do you understand?—*forever!* Should you be so unfortunate as to ever return here, should you be so unhappy as ever to emerge from your obscurity and cross my path, I will annihilate you. But before I annihilate you I will make you suffer the torments of hell, and wish that you had not been born. Do you understand?"

Oliver nodded his head.

"Very well, then, my child, we comprehend one another. Now I will show you Nicholas Jovus's mirror, which I told you was in my possession. It is a unique curiosity in its way."

He rose, and crossing the room to what appeared to be the door of a closet or cabinet, opened it, and showed within a hollow space, partly hidden by a curtain of some heavy black material. Oliver had followed him, and as the master drew back the curtain, he saw within an oval mirror, set in a heavy frame of copper.

"Now, Oliver," said the master, "what is it that you would wish to see?"

The thought of the perils from which he had escaped and the perils which still lay before him was uppermost in Oliver's mind. "I should like," said he, "to see that which will bring me the most danger in my life."

The master laughed. "It is a wise wish, my child," said he; "look and see."

He stood aside, and Oliver came forward and gazed into the glass. At first he saw nothing but his own face reflected clear and sharp as in an ordinary mirror; then suddenly, as he gazed, the bright surface of the glass clouded over as though with a breath blown upon it, and his own face faded away from his view. The next moment it cleared again, and he saw before him the face and form of a young lady, the most beautiful he had ever seen. He had only just time to observe that she sat in the window recess of what appeared to be a large and richly appointed room, and that she was reading a letter. Then all was gone—the master had dropped the curtain across the glass.

Oliver put his fingers to his forehead and looked about him, dazed and bewildered, for he felt as though he were going crazy in the presence of all the grotesque wonders through which he was passing.

The master also seemed disturbed. He frowned; he bit his lips; he looked at Oliver from under his brows. "Who is the young lady?" said he at last.

"I do not know," said Oliver, faintly. "I never saw her before."

"Here is a new complication," said the master. "One woman is more dangerous than a score of men." He brooded for a moment or two, and then his face cleared again. "No matter," said he; "we will not go to meet our difficulties, but will wait till they come to us. All the same, Oliver, take warning by one who knows that whereof he speaks. Avoid the women as you would a pitfall: they have been the ruin of many a better man. Remember that which I have told you of Raymond Lulli. He might perhaps have been living to-day, the richest and happiest man in the world, had he not been so stupid as to love Agnes de Villeneuve."

Oliver made no reply, but even while the other was uttering his warning he had determined in his own mind to seize the very first opportunity of looking again, and at his leisure, into the mirror, and to see again that danger which appeared in so alluring a form.

ACT II.

Scene First.—*An inn on the road to Flourens.*

A CALASH has lately arrived, and the horses are now being baited at the inn stables. The day is excessively warm and sultry, so that the young gentleman who came in the calash is having his bread, and a bottle of the wine for which the inn is famous, served to him under the great chestnut-tree before the door. It is Oliver Munier, but so different from the Oliver that left Paris a year before that even his mother would hardly have known him. He is no longer that peasant lad in blouse who crouched, shrunk together, in the corner of the great coach of the rich American uncle, being carried with thunderous rumble to some hideous and unknown fate which he did not dare to tell even to his own soul. He wore a silk coat, a satin waistcoat, satin breeches, silk stockings, a laced hat; he wore fine cambric cuffs at his wrists, and a lace cravat with a diamond solitaire at his throat, and his manners befitted his dress.

"THE INNKEEPER SERVED HIM IN PERSON."

He carried with him a small and curiously wrought iron box, of which he seemed excessively careful, keeping it close beside him, and every now and then touching it with his hand, as though to make sure that it had not been spirited away.

The innkeeper, a merry little pot-bellied rogue, as round as a dumpling and as red as an apple, served him in person, talking garrulously the while. Monsieur was on his way to Flourens? Ah! there was great excitement there to-day. What! Monsieur did not know? He must then be a stranger not to know that Monseigneur the Marquis had left Paris, and was coming back to the château to live.

Oliver was interested. He had seen monseigneur in Flourens once some two or three years before, when he had paid a flying visit to the château to put on another turn of the screw, and to squeeze all the money he could from the starving peasants of the estate, to pay some of his more hungry and clamorous creditors. All Flourens had known that the marquis was over head and ears in debt, and now the little gossiping landlord added the supplement. It was, he told Oliver, through no choice that Monseigneur the Marquis was to come back to the country again, but because he had no more wherewith to support his Paris life. He loathed Flourens, and he loved Paris; he hated the dull life of the country, and he adored the gayety of the city, its powder, its patches, its masques, its court, its vanity, its show, and, most of all, its intrigues and its cards. But all these cost money, for Monseigneur the Marquis had lived like a prince of the blood, and it had cost a deal. Ah, yes! such little matters as intrigues and the cards cost treasures of money in Paris, he had heard say. So now the marquis and the family were coming back again to Flourens.

By the time that the landlord had half done his gossip, Oliver had finished his bread and wine; then, the horses being refreshed, he bade the servant whom he had brought down from Paris with him to order out the calash. The landlord would have assisted Oliver in carrying his iron box, but Oliver would not permit it. He commanded him somewhat sharply to let it alone, and he himself stowed it safely within the calash.

His man-servant was holding the door open for him to enter, and Oliver already had his foot placed upon the step ready to ascend, when the clatter of hoofs and the rumble of a coach caught his attention, and he waited to see it pass.

It was a huge, lumbering affair, as big as a small

house, and was dragged thunderously along by six horses. A number of outriders surrounded it as it came sweeping along amid a cloud of dust, in the midst of which the whips of the postilions cracked and snapped like pistol-shots.

So Oliver waited, with some curiosity, until the whole affair had thundered by along the road, with its crashing, creaking, rattling clatter, preceded by the running footmen with their long canes, and the outriders in their uniform of white and blue. It was all gone in a moment— a moment that left Oliver standing dumb and rooted. In that instant of passing he had seen three faces through the open windows of the coach: the first, that of a stout, red-faced man, thick-lipped, sensual; second, that of a lady, pale and large-eyed, once beautiful perhaps, now faded and withered. But the third! The third face was looking directly at him, and it was the glimpse of it that left him rooted, bereft of motion. It was the same face that he had seen that first day in the magic mirror in the master's house; the face that he had seen in that mirror, and unknown to the master, not once, not twice, but scores of times—hundreds of times.

The landlord's voice brought him to himself with a shock. "Monsieur has dropped his handkerchief."

Oliver took the handkerchief mechanically from his hand, and as he entered the coach like one in a dream, he heard the landlord say, as his servant closed the door with a clash,

"That was Monseigneur the Marquis on his way to the Château Flourens."

Scene Second.—*The Widow Munier's house in Flourens. Not the poor rude hut that Oliver had left her in when he first went to Paris, but the house of the late Doctor Fouchette—the best house in the town. The Widow Munier is discovered sitting at the window, with her face close to the glass, looking down the street expectantly.*

Oliver had been gone a year, and that year had wrought great changes with her. All the town knew that a great fortune had come to her, and she was no longer the poor widow Munier, the relict of Jean Munier the tailor; she was Madame Munier.

After Oliver had been gone to Paris a week, there came a letter for her from him, and in the letter was money. Every week after came such another packet with more and more money— enough to lift her from poverty to opulence. She was no longer obliged to eat cabbage soup, or live in the poor little hut on the road. Just about that time Doctor Fouchette died, and, at

Oliver's bidding, she took the house for herself. It was very pleasant to her, but there was one thing that she could not understand. Her rich American brother-in-law had distinctly told her that he and Oliver were to go to Paris to choose a house, and that she was then to be sent for to live with them. She had never been sent for, and that was what she did not understand. Yet the weekly letters from Paris compensated for much. In those letters Oliver often told her that he and his uncle were in business together, and were growing rich at such a rate as no one had ever grown rich before. They were in the diamond business, he said, and in a little while he hoped to come home with more money than an East Indian prince. Then, at last, a little while after the twelvemonth had gone by, came a letter saying that he would be home upon the next Wednesday, in the afternoon. So now Madame Munier was sitting at the parlor waiting for that coming.

A calash came rattling along the stony street, and as it passed, the good people came to the doors and windows and looked after it. It did not stop at the inn, but continued straight along until it came to the door of Madame Munier's house. Then it drew up to the foot-way, and a servant in livery sprang to the ground and opened the door. A young gentleman stepped out, carrying an oblong iron box by a handle in the lid.

In thirty minutes all Flourens knew that Oliver Munier had returned home; in sixty minutes they knew he was as rich as Crœsus.

As Oliver released himself from his mother's embrace, he looked around him. It was all very different from the little hut on the road that he had left twelve months ago, but he seemed dissatisfied. He shook his head.

"It will never do," said he.

"What will never do?" said his mother.

"This house, this furniture—all," said Oliver, with a wave of his hand.

His mother stared. "It is a fine house," said she, "and the furniture is handsome. What, then, would you have?"

"The house is small; it is narrow; it is mean," said Oliver.

His mother stared wider than ever. "It is the best house in Flourens," said she.

"Perhaps," said Oliver; "but it does not please me. It will serve for us so long as we remain here, but I hope soon to remove to a better place—one more suitable for people of our condition."

Madame Munier's eyes grew as round as teacups. She began to notice that Oliver's manners and speech were very different from what they had been before he left Flourens a year ago. She herself had never used the barbarous Flourennaise patois.

"Remove to a better place?" she repeated, mechanically. "To one more suitable for people of our condition?"

"Yes," said Oliver. "I have in my mind a château in Normandy of which I have heard. I think of buying it."

Madame Munier's wonder had reached as high as it could soar. She began to wonder whether Oliver had not gone mad.

He gave her scarcely any time to recover before he administered another and a greater shock.

"Mother," said he, suddenly, "the family returns to the château to-day?"

"Yes," said his mother; "they passed through the town about a half an hour before you came."

"I know," said Oliver; "I saw them upon the road. There were two ladies with monseigneur. Do you know who they were?"

"One of them was thin and wrinkled, with black eyes and heavy eyebrows?"

"Yes," said Oliver.

"The other, a young girl, rather pretty?"

"She is beautiful!" said Oliver.

"No doubt they were Madame the Marquise, and Mademoiselle Céleste, the daughter," said Madame Munier.

There was a little time of silence, and then Oliver gave his mother that second shock, a shock such as the poor woman never had in her life before.

"Mother," said he, "I love Mademoiselle Céleste."

Madame Munier opened her eyes and mouth as wide as she was able. "You what?" she cried.

"I love Mademoiselle Céleste," said Oliver: it was delicious to repeat those words.

Madame Munier looked slowly all about her, as though she had dropped from the moon, and knew not as yet where she was. "He loves Mademoiselle Céleste!" she repeated to herself.

"Yes," said Oliver; "I love her."

"He loves her!" said Madame Munier, mechanically. "He is mad!"

"Mad!" said Oliver. "Why am I mad? Were I a beggar and she a princess I might still love her. Were I now as I was twelve months ago, poor, ignorant, dull, a witless, idle sot, satisfied to sit the day through on the bench in front of the inn yonder, I might still love her! Were we

"'MAD!' SAID OLIVER, 'WHY AM I MAD?'"

living in poverty as we were then—you and I—dwelling in that little stone hut, feeding upon stewed cabbage and onions, I might still love Céleste de Flourens! Love," cried Oliver—"love is universal; it is limitless; it is the right of every man, and no one can take it from him!"

Madame Munier listened; she thought that she had never heard any one talk so beautifully as Oliver. It put the matter in a new light.

"But I am no longer as I was then," continued Oliver. "I have seen much; I have passed through much; I have lived in Paris. But all would be of no importance were it not for another thing. Listen, mother! We are rich, you and I. We are the richest people in France—excepting one other; yes, the richest people in France! You think me crazy to love Céleste de Flourens! I tell you, I swear to you, I could to-morrow buy Flourens from one end to the other—the town, the château, and all. You do not believe me? Very well, you shall see! But as for this love of mine, it is not so hopeless nor so mad as you think. To-morrow you shall go in my coach, with my servant Henri, down to the château yonder."

"I shall do nothing of the sort," interrupted Madame Munier, sharply.

Oliver only smiled; he did not answer. A

habit he had caught from his master during the last year was to contradict nobody. "To-morrow you shall go down to the château in my coach, with my servant Henri, and then you shall see how complaisant the marquis will be."

"I shall do nothing of the sort," said Madame Munier again. "I will not go down to the château."

Still Oliver did not seem to hear her. Going to the table, he chose a key, and unlocking the iron box, brought forth from it a curious old silver snuffbox, handsomely chased and enamelled with figures and flowers. "Do you see this box?" said he, holding it up between his thumb and finger.

"Yes," said Madame Munier, "I see it; but I will not go to the château."

"It is only a snuffbox," said Oliver. "It is a small thing; but what then? Within it is a charm—a key with which I hope to unlock the portals of a new world to us. It shall give us the entrée to the château."

"I shall not go to the château," said Madame Munier.

"Also," said Oliver, "I will give you a letter, which you will present, together with this snuffbox, to the marquis; and I shall sign the letter Oliver de Monnière."

"But that is not your name," said Madame Munier.

"Very well," said Oliver; "but it shall hereafter be our name—yours and mine—De Monnière. Remember it, mother—De Monnière."

"But what, then, is in the snuffbox?" said Oliver's mother.

"I will show you," said Oliver, and he opened the lid.

"Bah!" said his mother; "and is that all? Do you think that Monseigneur the Marquis will care for that thing?"

Oliver smiled. "Yes," said he, "he will care for this thing."

Oliver's mother had nearly forgotten herself. "I will not go to the château," said she.

Scene Third.—*The marquis's apartments at the château.*

It is the next day after the marquis has returned to the Château de Flourens. It is three o'clock in the afternoon, and the marquis is discovered still in bed. His valet, August, an incomparable fellow, has been in and out a dozen times; has smoothed the marquis's clothes; has rearranged a freshly-powdered wig that hung as white as snow upon the block; has moved a chair here and a table there. But the Marquis de Flourens has paid no attention to him. He is reading the latest effusion of the immortal Jean Jacques; for one must keep up with the world, even if one is compelled to live in Flourens; moreover, as he often observes, a book suffices somewhat to relieve the ennui.

The Marquis de Flourens looks very droll. He is clad in a loose dressing-robe of figured cloth, and lies in bed reading his book, with a chocolate-pot and a delicate cup, with the brown dregs at the bottom, upon a light table standing at the bedside. His knees are drawn up into a little white mountain, the lace pillows are tucked in billowy masses behind him, and his nightcap is pushed a little to one side, giving a glimpse of his shining, newly-shaven head; his round face, in contrast with the white pillows behind, as red as a newly-risen sun.

The valet again enters the room, but this time with an object. He bears upon a silver tray a three-cornered billet and a snuffbox. The marquis lingeringly finishes the sentence he is reading, and then lays the book face down upon the bed beside him. "What is it you would have, August?" said he.

"A lady, monseigneur, has just now stopped at the door in a coach."

"HE IS CLAD IN A LOOSE DRESSING-ROBE OF FIGURED CLOTH, AND LIES IN BED READING HIS BOOK."

The marquis sat up as though moved by a spring. "A lady?" he cried. "Young, beautiful?"

"No," said August, seriously; "old, fat."

The marquis lay back upon the pillows again. "What is it that you have brought, August?" said he, languidly. August presented the waiter. "Oh!" said the marquis. "A letter; and what is that—a snuffbox?" He reached out and took Oliver's three-cornered billet from the waiter. "This is not a woman's handwriting," said he; "it is the handwriting of a man."

August said nothing, and the marquis opened the letter. It ran as follows:

"MONSEIGNEUR,—Having heard, monseigneur, that you have been interested in collecting odd and unique objects of curiosity and virtu, I have taken the great liberty of sending by madame my mother this insignificent trifle, which I hope, monseigneur, you will condescend to accept.
"OLIVER DE MONNIÈRE."

"M—m—m! What is it the fool is writing about? Curios? I making a collection of curios? I never collected anything in my life but debts. The man is crazy! Does he think that I am a snuffy collector of stuffy curios? Let me see the snuffbox, August."

The incomparable valet presented the waiter.

The marquis took the snuffbox in his hand and looked at it. "It is handsome," said he; "it is curious. It is solid silver, and is worth—" he weighed it in his hand—"a hundred livres, perhaps." He pressed the spring and opened the box as he spoke. It was full of cotton. Something dropped from it upon the coverlet. The marquis picked it up. It was a diamond of excessive brilliancy, almost as large as a bean.

The incomparable August was busied in removing the chocolate-pot and the empty cup, but presently observing the silence, he looked around. The marquis was holding something between his thumb and forefinger, and his eyes were as big as teacups. His face was a sight to see. August was startled out of his composure. He hastily set the waiter with the china upon the window-seat, and hurried to the bedside.

"What is it, monseigneur?" said he.

His voice roused the marquis.

"Where is the lady who came in the carriage?" he cried, excitedly. "Run, stop her!" He flung the bedclothes off himself and jumped with one bound out upon the floor.

Once again August was startled out of his decorum. "Monseigneur!" Then, recovering himself again: "The lady, monseigneur, is gone."

The gardener, working upon the terrace below, heard the rattle of a window flung violently open, and, upon looking up, was very much surprised to behold Monseigneur the Marquis, still clad in his colored dressing-gown, and with his nightcap thrust tipsily over one side of his head. So the marquis stood looking out of the window staring into space, for he had no more idea who it was that had stopped at the door and had left him a diamond worth twenty-five thousand livres than if he had never been born. "Ha!" thought he; "the letter; it was signed Oliver de Monnière." Thereupon he drew his head in and shut the window again.

SCENE FOURTH.—*The parlor of the house in Flourens.*

Oliver's mother has returned some little time from the château, and Oliver and she are talking it over between them.

"The marquis will visit us," said Oliver, "within an hour."

"He will do no such thing," said Oliver's mother; "he will not come at all."

"He will," said Oliver, taking out his brand-new watch from his breeches pocket and looking at it—"he will be here within a half an hour."

Oliver's mother sniffed incredulously. Oliver arose from the sofa where he was sitting and went to the window, and there stood drumming upon the sill, looking out into the street. Suddenly he drew back. The rumble of a coach was heard; it stopped before the house. A servant opened the coach door, and monseigneur himself stepped out.

He had driven over from the château, and had stopped at the inn. Pierre was standing at the door-way when the marquis leaned out from the window and beckoned—yes, actually beckoned to him. Pierre was so surprised that he took off not only his hat, but his wig also, and stood there bowing in the sun, with his head glistening like a billiard-ball.

"Do you know, innkeeper, of one Monsieur de Monnière who lives in this neighborhood?"

"Monsieur de Monnière?" repeated Pierre, blankly.

"Yes," said the marquis, impatiently. "De Monnière—Monsieur de Monnière. Do you know where Monsieur de Monnière lives?"

"Monsieur de Monnière," repeated Pierre, stupidly; he did not recognize the name.

The landlady stood in the door of the inn behind: woman are quicker of wit than men. "Monseigneur means Monsieur Oliver," said she.

The marquis overheard. "Yes," exclaimed he. "Monsieur Oliver— Monsieur Oliver de Monnière."

"Oh, Monsieur Oliver!" cried Pierre. "Oh yes, I know him as well as I know myself. He and his respected mother are now living up there on the hill. You can, monseigneur, see the house with your own eyes. It is that one with the white wall to the side, and with the apple and pear trees showing over the top. The rich Dr. Fouchette used to live there. It is, monseigneur, the finest house in Flourens. Monsieur Oliver indeed! That is good! I have known Monsieur Oliver ever since—"

But the coach was gone; the marquis had called out to the driver, had pulled up the window with a click, and now the coach was gone. Pierre stared after it for a while, and then he put on first his wig and then his hat, and went into the house again.

So Oliver drew back from the window and turned around. "You see, mother," said he, "monseigneur comes, as I asserted he would."

Oliver's mother was in a tremendous flutter. "And to think," said she, "of his coming all the way from the château just because of a little piece of cut-glass!"

Oliver laughed. "That little piece of cut-glass

was worth having," said he. "You do not yet know the value of little pieces of cut-glass like that, my mother."

Madame Munier did not listen to what Oliver was saying. "And to think," said she, "of Monseigneur the Marquis visiting me, the Widow Munier!"

"You forget, mother," said Oliver. "You are no longer Widow Munier, you are Madame de Monnière."

Henri opened the door. "The Marquis de Flourens," he announced; and the marquis entered the room with his feathered hat and his clouded cane in his hand.

"This is Monsieur Oliver de Monnière?" said he.

Oliver bowed.

"And this lady?"

"Permit me," said Oliver; "my mother."

Madame de Monnière courtesied so low that she nearly sat down upon the floor. She was profoundly agitated; she was frightened; she would rather be somewhere else. She was pleased. Yes, it was delicious having a marquis visit one in one's own house.

"And you, madame," said the marquis, "if I may be permitted to ask, did me the honor of calling upon me this morning?"

Madame de Monnière nodded. She was embarrassed at the thought of what she had done; she could not speak. Oliver spoke for her.

"She obliged me," said he, "by executing a little commission for me. Pardon me, monseigneur, that, knowing your interest as a collector, I took the liberty of sending a small specimen to you. I have your forgiveness?"

"Forgiveness!" exclaimed the marquis. "You ask me to forgive you? My dear child, I cannot accept such a gift. It is too great!"

"Do not speak so," said Oliver. "It is nothing—a trifle."

"Nothing!" cried the marquis; "a trifle! It is worth twenty-five thousand livres."

"What then?" said Oliver. "I have many others. You embarrass me by making so much of such a little thing. Let me beg that you will not refuse to accept of this trifle—as a connoisseur—as a collector of curios—"

"Ah!" said the marquis, "there you touch me —as a connoisseur—as a collector. Well, then, I accept it. But you—you say you have many others like this?—you are also a connoisseur?"

"Yes," said Oliver. "I have been indulging a very considerable taste in that direction for the past year. I think I may say now that I have as fine a collection of diamonds as any in Europe."

"Would that I might be permitted to see them!" said the marquis.

"You shall," said Oliver; "at least some of them. I can show you but a few at present. If you will pardon me for a moment, I will go and bring them."

He was gone, and Madame de Monnière and Monseigneur the Marquis were left alone together. For all this while the poor woman had been sitting dazed and bewildered. The words that had fallen upon her ears had overwhelmed her. That bit of glass—that little bit of cutglass—was worth twenty-five thousand livres! Twenty-five thousand livres! Monseigneur the Marquis himself had said so! Twenty-five thousand livres! and Oliver had given it to the marquis as a trifle! Twenty-five thousand livres! and she with her own ears had heard Oliver say that he had many more bits of glass like it! Yes, he had gone this very moment to bring them there and show them to the marquis. Twenty-five thousand livres! Was she dreaming or was she waking? Twenty-five thousand livres! She was amazed; she was bewildered; she was stupefied. In the midst of all, the marquis turned to her.

"And you, madame," said he, "why did you not wait this morning, and let me at least thank you for this magnificent gift?"

Madame de Monnière's head was spinning. "Twenty-five thousand livres!" said she.

"Ah, I see," said the marquis. "You are embarrassed at the considerableness of it. It is, indeed, from one point of view, a treasure; but we connoisseurs, madame, we collectors, we frequently exchange these little precious curiosities. It is our habit."

Madame de Monnière rose for a moment to the surface of her bewilderment. "Yes," said she; "that is true;" and thereupon sank again into the gulf. "Twenty-five thousand livres!" she murmured to herself.

Just then Oliver returned. In his hand he carried a small box of curiously-wrought iron. Unlocking it, he raised the lid, removed a layer of cotton, and then, tilting it, emptied upon the table a handful of diamonds, that fell flashing and sparkling like broken fragments of sunlight. One or two of the gems rolled across the table and fell hopping to the floor, but Oliver did not appear to notice them. There was a pause of blank and utter silence. Madame de Monnière herself could not have been more amazed at the sight she beheld than was the Marquis de Flourens. Oliver spread out the gems upon the table with his hand, as though they were so many glass beads.

It was the marquis who broke the silence. "Mon Dieu!" he whispered at last, and fetched a breath so deep that it seemed to come from the pit of his stomach. Then he roused himself. "You have dropped some upon the floor," said he. "I saw them fall." And he would have stooped to find them.

Oliver smiled. "It is of no importance," said he. "Henri will find them by-and-by."

For a while the marquis examined the stones in silence, picking out some of the larger gems, and scrutinizing them closely and critically, one after another. "It is a most magnificent collection, my young friend," said he at last. "I never saw a finer lot of diamonds in my life, excepting the King's."

"Oh, these are but a few," said Oliver. "I am sorry that I have not some of my larger and finer stones to show you."

"Only a few?" repeated the marquis. "And how much, then, do you suppose that this collection of diamonds is worth?"

"That would be hard to tell," said Oliver, smiling. "But perhaps not more than half a million livres. None of the stones are very large or fine."

"OLIVER SPREAD OUT THE GEMS UPON THE TABLE WITH HIS HAND."

"Not large? Not fine?" cried the marquis, and he picked out a diamond from among the rest. "What, then, do you call this?"

"It is off color," said Oliver.

"It is a treasure that a king might covet!" cried the marquis, enthusiastically.

Oliver laughed. "You admire it?" said he. "Then do me the favor to accept it."

The marquis rose to his feet. "Oh," he cried, "this is too much! I do not dare."

"You pain me by refusing," said Oliver. "As a connoisseur, monseigneur, as a collector—"

"Ah!" said the marquis, "there you touch me again. As a collector—well, then, I accept it," and he slipped it into his waistcoat pocket. "Embrace me, Oliver!"

Oliver's mother was long past wondering at anything, or else she might have thought it a little strange to see Oliver—Oliver, the son of Jean Munier, the tailor—clasped in the arms of Monseigneur the Marquis of Flourens.

The marquis released Oliver from his embrace and sat down again. "But tell me," said he, "you and madame, you then live here?"

He looked around, and Oliver's eyes followed his. It certainly was a poor house for one who could empty half a million livres' worth of diamonds upon a table.

"For the present," said Oliver, "yes. We have been very poor, my mother and I." He paused. The marquis's eyes were resting intently upon him, and he felt that the other waited for further explanation. He had already arranged a story, but now that the time had come to tell it, his courage almost failed. "My uncle," said he at last, "came back from America about a year ago, and found us very poor—my mother and me. He was rich." Again he paused for a moment, and then continued: "He came from Brazil, where he was the owner of a diamond mine."

"But this uncle of yours," said the marquis, "where is he now?"

"He is dead," said Oliver. "He is in heaven."

Oliver's mother heard what he said through all the buzzing of the thoughts in her head. "So, then," thought she to herself, "my brother-in-law is dead, is he?"

"And you?" said the marquis.

"I?" said Oliver. "I have inherited his fortune. It is all in diamonds."

Madame Munier pricked up her ears. She was growing interested. Her Oliver, then, had inherited a fortune.

"And your uncle's name—what was it?" said the marquis.

"His name?" said Oliver. "His name was Henri, the Chevalier de Monnière-Croix."

"The devil!" whispered Oliver's mother to herself. "I did not know that we were so well connected." She was past being surprised at anything now.

"De Monnière-Croix?" repeated the marquis. "De Monnière-Croix? The name is not familiar."

"Perhaps not," said Oliver. "My uncle was very young—a mere child—when he went to America, and for the twelve months past since his return to France he and I have been living quietly together in Paris, where he was engaged in settling his affairs."

The marquis was looking steadily at him. "Is your family of long descent?" said he.

"Not very; as I said, my father was very poor; you know, monseigneur, how sadly poor people of good family may be in the country—" He hesitated, and then stopped.

"But," said the marquis, presently, "you say your uncle is dead. Had he, then, no other heirs than you? Had he no children?"

"No," said Oliver.

"And you inherit all—*all* his wealth?"

"All."

"It is then considerable?"

"It is one of the greatest fortunes in France."

"Can you prove that to me?"

"I can."

"Embrace me, my dear child!"

As the marquis rode back again to the château he sat in the corner of the coach, meditating deeply over all that he had seen and heard. "The Chevalier de Monnière-Croix," he muttered to himself—"the Chevalier de Monnière-Croix." Then he suddenly aroused himself from his meditations, thrust his thumb and finger into his waistcoast pocket, and drew out the diamond that Oliver had given him. He held it in a dozen different lights, examining it keenly and critically. Finally he thrust it back again into the pocket whence he had taken it. "At least," said he, "his diamonds are real. Why, then, should he not be of noble family if he chooses? A half a million livres' worth of diamonds, and that, as he tells me, only a small part of his wealth! Very well, then, his uncle was a chevalier and he is a prince—the Prince de Golconda, if he chooses."

Oliver stood for a long while looking out of the window after the marquis's coach had driven away. He felt very uneasy; he wished that he had not told those lies; they frightened him. He felt as if he could see them already flying home again to roost. But he need not have been afraid. And then, besides, if there was a cloud, it had had a silver edge: the last words that the marquis had uttered had been: "My dear Oliver, let me hope that we may soon see you at the château—you and your mother" (that was an after-thought), "for my daughter Céleste will find it very stupid with no young people about. I shall not, however, be able to show you my collection of diamonds, unfortunately; they are at present—ahem!—in Paris."

Scene Fifth.—*A garden at the Château de Flourens.*

A garden such as Watteau loved to paint—bosky trees, little stretches of grassy lawn, white statues of nymphs and fauns peering from among the green leaves, a statue of a naiad pouring water from a marble urn, green with moss, into a marble basin, green with moss.

In front of all, the smooth river, dusked and dappled now and then by little breezes that slowly sway the tops of the tall poplar-trees. The little birds sing, and patches of sunlight and shadow flicker upon the grass.

Enter Oliver and Mademoiselle Céleste. She carries a pink parasol that makes her face glow like a rose leaf, and Oliver walks by her side.

That morning Oliver had paid his first visit to the château. His master had trained him well in the ways of the world during the twelvemonth he had lived with him in Paris; nevertheless, he came to the château quivering with trepidation. But now the trepidation had passed and gone, and it was all like the bewildering glamour of some strange dream—the presence of his love no longer dumbly reflected from the smooth, passionless mirror, but in warm living flesh and blood, breathing and articulate. She spoke; she smiled; it was divine. A little wind blew a gauze of hair across her soft cheek now and then as they walked together; her sleeve brushed against Oliver's arm, and Oliver's heart quivered and thrilled.

That night was to him but a succession of dreams, coming one after another like a continuous panorama, only each separate picture centred in one figure, and Oliver himself walked along beside her, and told her that he loved her. It was a deliciously restless night.

After Oliver had gone home, the marquis lingered for a moment or two in madame's apartment, standing with his back to the fireplace listening while she talked to him.

"I do not like him," said she; "he is ostentatious. Who ever heard of wearing diamond knee

"ENTER OLIVER AND MADEMOISELLE CÉLESTE."

and shoe buckles in the country? The solitaire pin in his cravat was enormous."

"It was a magnificent diamond," said the marquis.

"He is an adventurer," replied the marquise.

The marquis felt in his waistcoat pocket, and brought out the two diamonds that Oliver had given him. He held them in the palm of his hand under the nose of the marquise. "Bah!" said he; "you talk like a fool, Matilde. Do adventurers, then, give away seventy-five thousand livres' worth of diamonds as though they were chestnuts? Did you ever hear of an adventurer who carried around a half a million livres' worth of diamonds in a little box? No; he may not be an aristocrat, but he is certainly an Aladdin."

So Oliver was made welcome at the château whenever he chose to come. By the time that a month had passed, he had grown into a certain intimacy. They all liked him; even madame had condoned his diamonds and liked him. Then one morning the marquis received an astounding letter from his protégé.

"Monseigneur," it said, "I recognize in you a true and kind friend, a man of the world upon whom I can depend." (Oliver's master in Paris had done wonders for him; he really wrote very well.) "I am, monseigneur, troubled and harassed. I am young and without experience. I now have with me here my whole fortune, which consists entirely of diamonds—the gleaning of years from my American uncle's mines in Brazil. I do not think that I overestimate, monseigneur, in saying that that fortune is worth—" (I will not repeat what the figures were, they were so tremendous, so unbelievable, that the marquis laid the letter down, and gazed around him bewildered. "If this is true," said he, drawing a deep breath, "my young friend is the richest man in France." Thereupon he picked up the letter, and read the figures over again, and then over again. "He must have made a mistake of a cipher," said the marquis. But no; the amount was not only given in numbers, but written out in full—there could be no mistake. The marquis resumed the reading of the epistle.) "I am," continued the letter, "tormented with fears at having this vast amount in my house"—"I should think so," muttered the marquis to himself—"which, though at present a profound secret, may at any time be discovered. What dangers I would then be in, I leave you to judge for yourself. I have, monseigneur, no friends, no relatives, of sufficient age and experience to advise me in my difficulties. Accordingly I turn to you, who have shown me so much kindness, and beseech you that you will so far continue it—I may say increase it—as to take charge of this treasure, and advise me as to how I may best dispose of it."

Such was the matter of Oliver's letter. The Marquis de Flourens sat for a long while meditating very deeply and seriously upon what he had read. That same morning Oliver received a note from him, "Bring your little fortune, my child," it said. "What a father may do for a son, I will do for you."

SCENE SIXTH.—*The marquis's cabinet. The marquis discovered seated at a table, drumming upon it with his fingers, and awaiting the coming of Oliver, who has just been announced. Enter Oliver, carrying a stout iron-bound box, which he deposits upon the table.*

"Your treasure is in that box?" says the marquis.

Oliver nodded. He was very pale.

The marquis arose, and not only locked the door, but even covered the key-hole from the drilling of inquisitive eyes.

"Now, my dear child," said he, turning to Oliver with a smile, "let us see what we have in our box;" and he drew his chair again to the table beside which Oliver was standing.

They were both of them agitated — the marquis from expectancy, and Oliver from the great cast of the die of his life, which he had determined that day to make. The hand with which he unlocked the box was as cold as ice.

The contents of the box was covered with a layer of cotton. Oliver removed it, and then by two straps lifted out a shallow wooden tray covered with purple velvet, and filled with a glittering mass of diamonds of the purest water, nearly all of them large and fine. The marquis's eyes gleamed as brightly as the stones themselves.

Below the tray was another layer of cotton. Oliver removed it and then another tray; then another layer of cotton and another tray, until there were eight of them spread upon the table — it could hold no more.

"There are two more trays in the box," said Oliver, "but it is not necessary that I should show you them; these are sufficient."

The marquis did not reply; he was overwhelmed by what he beheld; it seemed to him that he saw the treasures of Golconda. Oliver observed his silence, and, looking up, saw that his face had grown white with the intensity of his emotions. At last he drew a deep breath, and raised his eyes to Oliver's; then feeling in his pocket, he drew forth his handkerchief and wiped his face. His voice was husky when he spoke. "But this vast, this unbelievable treasure," said he, "what security shall I give you if you intrust it to me to manage for you?"

The opportunity for Oliver's *coup* had arrived. The marquis himself had given him the very chance which he sought, but now that he was face to face with it, he trembled, he hesitated, he feared to put his happiness to the test of speech. Yet he knew that now or never was the time to cast the die of his hopes upon the table of fate. He braced himself, gathered all the force of his will, and as the blinding rush of resolution overwhelmed him, he saw only the marquis's face and the marquis's eyes looking into his.

"Your security," said he, hoarsely — and his voice sounded in his ears as though it was not his own — "your security — let it — let it be — your daughter."

The words were spoken. There came a long pause of deep, intense silence, through which Oliver could hear the throbbing blood singing in his ears. The marquis never moved a hair, but sat looking into Oliver's eyes. Oliver felt a dry, hard lump gather in his throat; he tried to swallow it. The marquis pushed back his chair and arose. Oliver's eyes dumbly followed his motion. The marquis began walking up and down the room, but he did not say "No." After a while he stopped before one of the windows and there stood a while, with his hands clasped behind him, looking out upon the lawn and the river beyond. Minute after minute passed in a straining tensity of silence. Oliver began to feel as though he could bear it no longer. Suddenly the marquis spoke:

"My daughter?" said he, half aloud and half to himself. The words meant nothing, but they were not words of refusal. Oliver felt a great wave of blinding hope sweep over him. Suddenly the marquis turned and came back to the table. He motioned Oliver to a chair. "Let us talk this matter over," said he, seriously, and they both sat down. Oliver's heart thumped within him like a trip-hammer. "Do you know," said the marquis, "what a thing it is that you ask? Do you know that you ask an alliance with one of the noblest houses of France?" Oliver could not answer. "And you," continued the marquis, "who are you? I do not know you; nobody knows you. You may be what you represent yourself to be; you may be an adventurer."

Oliver's heart was sinking like a plummet of lead. "My diamonds are real," he croaked.

The marquis smiled, and then a long space of

"'DO YOU KNOW,' SAID THE MARQUIS, 'WHAT A THING IT IS THAT YOU ASK?'"

silence fell. At last he spoke again, and his words shot through Oliver's heart like a dart. "What settlement, then, would you propose to make upon your wife?" said he.

"Wife!" Oliver's heart thrilled with the sudden keenness of that pang of sharp delight. His brain whirled in an eddy of dizzy light. At last, with a supreme effort, he found his tongue. "Anything," he cried—"anything that you choose!"

The marquis smiled again. "We are ardent," said he. "I see that if this matter is to be carried forward, I must act not only as a father, but as a friend. I confess to you, Oliver, that I am deeply in debt, that Flourens is mortgaged to the last inch. Would you be willing to release Flourens, and then settle the estate upon your wife?"

"Yes," said Oliver, eagerly.

The marquis's smile grew wider than ever. "That is good," said he. "But you must know that you are one of the richest men in France, Oliver. You should do even more than that for your wife."

"I will settle upon her everything that I have in the world," said Oliver.

The marquis laughed. "Ah!" said he, "we are certainly too ardent—far too ardent. Half of your fortune would be sufficient; or three-quarters of it, at the most."

"She shall have either, as you may choose," said Oliver.

"I suppose," said the marquis, "that it will be best that I should manage her fortune for her?"

"Yes," said Oliver. "And you shall manage mine also, if you choose."

The marquis saw that there was no limit to Oliver's complacency. "And you will subscribe to that?" said he.

"Yes," said Oliver. "I am willing to subscribe to anything."

The marquis rose from the chair, and opened his arms. "Embrace me, my son," said he.

Oliver could have cried with happiness. "And may I," said he, tremulously, when the marquis had released him from his arms—"may I then—" He hesitated; he could not believe that he had reached such a dizzy pinnacle of happiness.

The marquis laughed. "You will find mademoiselle in the garden," said he.

Scene Seventh.—*The Watteau-like garden described before— the trees, the statues, the fountains, the flowers, the river. Mademoiselle Céleste is discovered sitting in the shade, reading, and making just such a picture as the great artist would have painted upon a fan.*

Enter Oliver, running down the steps of a terrace, dizzy with joy, like one in the bewildering glamour of a golden dream. He seemed to tread upon air! The blue sky, green foliage, the flowers, the statues, the rivers, swam together in a confusion of bewildered delight. At the sound of his footsteps she raises her eyes, and lays aside her book, and greets him with the smile of an acquaintance.

"Oh!" said she; "it is you, then? I have been waiting for you."

Oliver's heart was fluttering within him. At first he could not speak, and she must have read his joy and his secret in his face, for the rosy hue upon her cheeks deepened.

He sank upon his knees beside her. "I love you," he whispered, tremulously.

Her face was turned away from him, but she did not withdraw the hand which he held. There was a long time of silence. Oliver raised her hand to his lips.

"But my father," she murmured at last.

"He bade me seek you here," cried Oliver, eagerly. Then again: "Oh, Céleste, I love you! I love you!"

She turned her face towards him; her eyes met his then. Could he believe it? Was it real? His lips met others, soft, warm, fragrant. The flowers, the parterres, the trees, the blue sky, the white marble statues—all dissolved into a golden ether. Flourens? **It was heaven!**

Madame the Marquise made no objection to it all. She had become accustomed to Oliver and his diamonds. He was a pleasant, cheerful, handsome fellow. It made her heart feel lighter to have him about. As was said, she had forgiven the ill taste of the display of diamonds, and now expressed her approval of the arrangement. Oliver's heaven was without a cloud.

SCENE EIGHTH.—*The marquis's private closet.*

A month had passed—a month of delight, of joy, of love; and then one morning the Marquis de Flourens let fall a torpedo in the midst of Oliver's little paradise. That morning, when Oliver went to the château, the marquis sent for him. Oliver found him seated at the table, play-

"HE SANK ON HIS KNEES BESIDE HER."

ing idly with a gold pencil-case. He did not ask Oliver to be seated, but went directly to the point.

"A week from next Monday," said he, "we shall go to Paris. You also, my dear Oliver."

Oliver stood like one stunned. He made no answer, but his mind, in a single sweep, cleared the whole horizon. To Paris! He remembered the master's commands—those commands so terribly absolute; he remembered his threats of punishment if he (Oliver) should disobey that mandate. What was that threat? Oliver remembered it well. It was that that terrible mysterious being, who had so nearly doomed him to a dreadful, unspeakable death, would crush him, would annihilate him, would make him wish a thousand times, in his torments, that he had never been born. Those were almost the very words, and Oliver had not forgotten them. He had learned much of his master in the year that he had lived with him, and he knew that that threat was not idle. He knew that the master would do as he said to the last jot and tittle. That cool, smiling, sinister devil! He could destroy all of this happiness as easily as one can destroy a beautiful soap-bubble that a child has created from nothing.

"I do not wish to go to Paris," said Oliver, huskily.

The marquis's face darkened. "Not wish to go to Paris?" he repeated. " But **you** must go, Oliver."

"No," said Oliver; "I do not wish to go. I shall not go. I would rather stay here at Flourens. I do not like Paris."

The marquis came over and took Oliver by the button of his coat. His face was not pleasant to see. "You do not like Paris!" said he. "Very well; then you shall stay here, my dear Oliver—you and your fortune. But in that case, my child, you need never come here to the château again. You comprehend me?"

Oliver looked out of the window. Céleste was waiting for him upon the terrace. Never had she looked so exquisitely beautiful. He groaned.

"Then I will go," said he.

The marquis opened his arms. "Embrace me, Oliver," he cried.

Oliver yielded himself to the caress, but he wished the marquis to the devil.

ACT III.—Paris.

Scene First.—*Madame de Pompadour's salon.*

Some dozen courtiers, male and female, are gathered in a group at a little distance, but not too far away, from a sofa standing by an open window, just where the breeze comes in pleasantly from without. A lady dressed in negligee *robe de chambre* of blue satin lies upon the sofa, propped up with pillows. She is slowly fanning herself with a very charmingly painted fan, listening the while impassively to the subdued talk, and the occasional ripple of laughter that follows some more than usually apt observation or repartee. She does not talk or smile herself, but only continues fanning herself with slow impassiveness. She is still beautiful, but she is somewhat haggard and worn, and even the powder and rouge, and an occasional patch here and there, cannot altogether hide the leaden pallor of ill health. It is Madame de Pompadour, and it is one of the days in which she feels more than usually unwell.

The conversation of those around chiefly concerns two lovers, whom all Paris is just now petting and caressing, the young and charming Monsieur de Monnière-Croix and his fiancée Mademoiselle de Flourens. The match is altogether a singular and remarkable one. Those who have seen the young man report him very handsome, but it is whispered that he is of obscure origin. Were it not for his stupendous wealth, the story of which is very well authenticated, it would have been a dreadful misalliance. As it is, that wealth is so great as to level all distinctions, and the world has not only forgiven the match, but has been vastly interested in the love affair. The talk of it has reached even Madame de Pompadour's ears, and she has been pleased to express a desire to have them presented to her. The day and the time for that presentation has arrived, and that perhaps is why the conversation just now concerns the lovers.

Madame de Berry protests that they are the handsomest couple that she has ever seen; their love so innocent, so deliciously childlike. They are a new Corydon and Phyllis—Cupidon and Psyche. In them Arcadia is come again. It is the prettiest thing in the world to see their uneasiness when separated, their fond glances when together.

Monsieur de Gontat had heard the Duchesse de Choiseul speak of them the other day. She declares them her latest passion, and says that they are like that which the poets describe, and which nobody ever saw before. She loves to have them near her—the dear Duchesse—and says that they make her feel that life is not altogether like the new screen that Monsieur Watteau has just finished for her, not altogether flat, not altogether surface, not all pretended simplicity in powder and patches, and with painted fan to hide a painted blush; she says they make her have a better opinion of herself. So the buzz of talk goes on, and Madame de Pompadour fans herself and listens impassively.

Then the talk suddenly turns to the Count de St. Germaine, who has grown such a favorite, not only with Madame de Pompadour, but of late with his Majesty himself.

Monsieur de Gontat tells of the last wonder relating to him. Yesterday his Majesty sent for him.

"Monsieur Count," said he, "they say that you can remove flaws from a diamond. Is it so?"

"Yes, sire," answered the count.

"Then here is a diamond that would be worth fifty thousand livres except for this flaw; it is not worth five thousand now. Can you remedy it?"

"I can try, sire," answers the count, and he slips it into his waistcoat.

Would you believe it? He brings it in this morning sound and whole and without flaw.

"I myself," says Monsieur de Gontat, "was present when the jeweller appraised it. His Majesty said that he would keep it as one of the greatest curiosities of his cabinet."

Monsieur de Gontat had hardly ended his story when Oliver and Céleste were announced.

Madame de Pompadour ceased her fanning and turned her head languidly as they were ushered across the room and presented.

The Marquis de Flourens, who had come with them, was also presented. He paid his respects, and then immediately withdrew to one side, and was absorbed in the little group of those in waiting.

Madame reached out her hand to Céleste. "Come hither, my child, and let me look at you," said she.

Céleste came timidly forward, and Madame de Pompadour took her by the hand. She drew her down until the girl kneeled upon the floor beside the sofa. The poor sick woman looked long and earnestly into her young face.

"You are beautiful, you are young, you are happy," she murmured. "You are happy, are you not?"

"SHE DREW HER DOWN UNTIL THE GIRL KNEELED UPON
THE FLOOR BESIDE HER."

"Yes," answered Céleste, in a whisper.

"And you love Monsieur de Monnière-Croix?"

"Yes," whispered Céleste again, and her voice thrilled.

Madame de Pompadour fetched a little half-sigh, which faded to a smile before it had left her lips. "Ah!" said she, "it is the young who are happy." Then, after a moment's pause, "Will you kiss me, child?"

Céleste bent forward, and her fresh young innocent lips met those others—so soiled, so wan and faded. It was all as effectively done as anything upon the boards of the Comédie Française.

Madame de Pompadour turned with a smile, and beckoned to Oliver.

"Come, Monsieur Count," said she, "your place should be here beside your lady;" and she motioned to him to kneel beside Céleste.

Oliver saw the ladies and gentlemen who stood around smile. He was embarrassed; he blushed like a school-boy; but there was nothing for him to do but to kneel. Céleste saw his confusion, and furtively reached out her little hand and gave his an encouraging squeeze. Madame de Pompadour saw it and smiled. Yes, it certainly was Arcadian.

At that moment another arrival was announced, "Monsieur the Count de St. Germaine!"

Now and then the name of the Count de St. Germaine, and the story of his strange doings, reached even to the paradise of the lovers. Occasionally Oliver heard a breath of these things, and when he heard it he trembled—the breath was sinister and smelt from the pit. But he was not troubled for long at a time; his cockle floated gayly along the stream of fateful happiness; he was too absorbed in his love-dreams to burden his thoughts with the fear of being overwhelmed in the dark waters upon which that cockle swam. Nevertheless, the name, falling so unexpectedly upon Oliver's ears, came with a certain shock of dread. He bent his head as he kneeled, and for a time did not dare to look around. The new-comer came forward with the well-assured air of a favorite. Oliver could feel him coming nearer and nearer.

"Rise, my children," said Madame de Pompadour. And as they obeyed, she presented Oliver to the other. "Monsieur de St. Germaine," said she, "let me present to you Monsieur de Monnière-Croix."

Oliver slowly raised his eyes, and then his heart crumbled away within him. *It was the master!*

It seemed to Oliver as though the room darkened around him, and he saw but one thing—

"MONSIEUR THE COUNT DE ST. GERMAINE!"

that cold, handsome face. His ears rang as though with a chime of bells. The floor seemed to rock beneath his feet, for he knew what to expect when those thin lips parted—he would be denounced, exposed, here before Madame de Pompadour and her court. His heart shrunk together, but he steeled himself to face the coming blow.

But he was mistaken. The thin lips parted, the face lit up with a smile. "Ah," cried the well-known voice, "it is Oliver; it is the little Oliver! You do not remember me. No? Oh, well, it is not likely you would; and yet I was the dearest friend that your poor uncle, who is now in Paradise, had in the world." He turned to the others who stood there, still holding Oliver by the hand, which he had taken when he first began speaking. "The world," said he, "does not yet know half the romance connected with this young man. His uncle Henri, Chevalier de Monnière-Croix, was one of the richest men in France. Poor soul! he is dead now, but when he lived he was the owner of one of the largest diamond mines in Brazil. Diamonds! The world has never seen the like of the Chevalier de Monnière-Croix's diamonds! And now this young man has been left heir to them all. Henri de Monnière-Croix and I were in Brazil together, and it was with him that I gained what little knowledge I possess concerning precious stones; I may say, indeed, that he was my teacher in that knowledge. I was intimately acquainted with his affairs, and know that Oliver, as is reputed of him, is one of the richest men in Europe."

All who were present listened to the count's speech with breathless interest and in dead silence. But to Oliver the words he heard spoken lifted him at a bound from the gulf of despair into which he was falling. The master did not mean to ruin him just then. The rebound from the tensity of the strain was too great for him to bear. The ground beneath his feet heaved and rocked, the room spun around and around. He heard some one, he knew not whom, give a sharp exclamation; he felt a strong, sinewy arm clasp him about the body; he knew it was the master's arm, and then—nothing.

SCENE SECOND. — *A room in the Hotel de Flourens, whither Oliver has been removed after having fainted in madame's salon.*

It is the next day, and Oliver is discovered lying upon a sofa, limp, heart-sick, overshadowed by the looming of coming misfortune. The ladies have sent many inquiries as to his health, and two little notes from Céleste are lying upon the table at his elbow. Enter suddenly Henri, who is in attendance upon him.

"A gentleman to see monsieur," said the valet, and almost instantly another voice, speaking from behind him, said:

"It is I, Oliver. I have taken the liberty of an old friend of your dear uncle; I was anxious concerning your health, and so followed immediately. You need not wait, Henri"—to the valet.

He entered as he spoke, and waiting for a moment to make sure that Henri had gone, then closed the door and turned to Oliver, who now sat speechless, motionless, fascinated, with eyes fixed, and a face as white as wax. He drew forward a chair, and placing it close to Oliver, sat for a long time looking fixedly and intently at him. At last, without removing his eyes, he drew out his snuffbox—the famous snuffbox that Madame de Pompadour had given him with her own hands —and took a pinch of snuff with a deal of gusto.

"Well," said he, "have you nothing to say to me?"

"I thought," said Oliver, dully, "that it was you who had, perhaps, something to say to me."

The Count de St. Germaine laughed. "Something to say to you?" said he. "Oh! You mean, perhaps, about that looking-glass of mine, upon which you drew that accursed sign with one of those very diamonds that I had taught you to make? Perhaps you thought that by doing so you would prevent my following your motions for the future. Well, as far as the mirror is concerned, you were right; you have spoiled it for me. You, who are generally so dull, sometimes surprise one with sudden gleams of your bucolic cunning. I confess that you did most effectually what you intended; you ruined that looking-glass forever. So far as I am concerned, I can never see anything in it again. Are you not deserving of punishment for that?"

Oliver strove to speak, but his white lips uttered no sound.

"Again," said the Count de St. Germaine, "I commanded you when we parted that you should never return to Paris; I forbade you imperatively, absolutely, from coming. I unbosomed myself to you and told you all; I confessed to you that I feared your influence upon my destiny. What has resulted? You, knowing that you have taken away all my means of following your movements, did return here against those express commands that I had laid upon you,

"THE COUNT DE ST. GERMAINE, WITHOUT REMOVING HIS EYES FROM HIS VICTIM, TOOK ANOTHER DEEP, LUXURIOUS PINCH OF SNUFF."

braving all my threats of punishment. Should you not be punished for that?"

"I could not help it," said Oliver, hoarsely; "the marquis compelled me to come."

Once more the other laughed. "I know nothing of that," said he. "I only know that you are here. Why you are here concerns yourself, and not me. Now what do you think that I am about to do to you, Oliver?"

"I do not know," said Oliver. And he hid his face in his trembling hands.

The Count de St. Germaine, without removing his eyes from his victim, took another deep, luxurious pinch of snuff. Then he shut the lid with a snap, and slipped the box again into his pocket, but all that time his eyes never once moved from the cowering Oliver. Suddenly he burst out laughing, and clapped the lad upon the shoulder. "I will tell you what I will do to you, Oliver," said he; "I will forgive you! Do you hear me? *I will forgive you!*"

Oliver slowly removed his hands from his face, and looked up with dumb bewilderment. "You forgive me?" he repeated, stupidly.

"Yes, I forgive you."

A long pause of silence followed, during which Oliver looked intently and earnestly into that smiling face, so close to his own. That smiling face—it was an impenetrable mask, it was the face of a sphinx, and Oliver might almost as well have tried to read the one as the other. Yet there was a soul behind it, and that soul could not entirely be hidden; one glimpse of it flashed out through the eyes. Oliver saw it and shuddered.

"You forgive me?" he repeated. "What do you mean? I do not comprehend. What would you have me do?"

The other shrugged his shoulders and raised his eyebrows. "What would I have you do?" said he. "You surprise me! I talk to you, and you do not seem to hear me. I say that I forgive you, and you do not seem to understand. What I mean is that you shall continue to live here, as you have already done, in an atmosphere of happiness and love. It is beautiful, as all Paris says; it is delightful! After all, I cannot punish you, for I have not the heart to interfere with it. By-and-by you shall marry Mademoiselle Céleste."

Oliver never removed his looks from the other's face. "Marry Céleste?" he murmured, mechanically.

"Certainly," said the other, "I never saw you so dull. I said that you were to marry Mademoiselle Céleste—to marry her. But, there!

I see what it is. You are not yet recovered from your illness in Madame de Pompadour's salon. It was indeed insufferably hot. Poor lady! she is like a green cockatoo, she cannot abide a touch of cold. But I weary you; I will take another opportunity of visiting you. But remember, my dear Oliver, I forgive you. *Au revoir!*"

He was gone; and Oliver sat as Monsieur de St. Germaine had left him, clad in his dressing-gown, and seated upon the edge of the sofa, leaning with his elbows upon his knees, his hands clasped before him, and his eyes fixed dully upon the floor. Forgive him! His soul told him that he need expect no forgiveness from that cold, iron heart. What should he do? How should he escape the fate which he felt was hanging over him? The master had said that he was to marry Céleste. Upon the eve of that marriage, perhaps, he would come and proclaim him the cheat, the charlatan that he was. He shuddered as he pictured the shame of the humiliation of such a disclosure. Suddenly a thought flashed upon him, like light upon the darkness: why not tell Céleste his story? Why not confess all to her, and throw himself upon her mercy? His shame would be less, and she would scorn him less, than if he waited for the Count de St. Germaine to expose him. His heart stood still at the thought of Céleste's grief and despair. And Paris! How Paris would laugh at the denouement of that romance which it now petted and approved. In a sudden rush of determination, and without giving himself time for second thought, he drew paper and ink towards him, and set himself to write a letter to Céleste. It was a blundering, blotted letter. It took him a long, long time to write it, but at last it was done; in it he told her all; and then, still without giving himself time to think, he rang the bell, and Henri appeared. He hesitated, for one last moment, with a shrinking heart.

"What will monsieur have?" said Henri.

"Take this letter," said Oliver, with one last, desperate resolve, "to Mademoiselle Céleste, and—and wait her answer."

"Yes, monsieur."

Oliver watched the man as he crossed the room, as he noiselessly closed the door; he was gone.

How long the answer was in returning Oliver never could tell. It might have been only a few minutes that he walked up and down the room. It seemed to him hours.

"Monsieur, a letter."

Oliver turned sharply. It was Henri, and he

presented upon his tray a little note. It was, as far as outward appearance was concerned, almost exactly like those two others upon the table; but what was within? Oliver hardly dared touch it. He opened it slowly, hesitatingly; there were only three words, "I love you"—that was all. Yes, that was all. Oliver sat looking at it with eyes that blinded more and more, until at last one hot drop fell with a pat upon the open sheet. Then even Henri's presence was not enough to inspire self-control. He broke down, and began crying, and probably, if Henri thought anything at all, it was that there had been a quarrel.

SCENE THIRD.—*The grand salon of the Hôtel de Flourens; the hour, near midnight. Oliver is discovered walking rapidly and agitatedly up and down the length of the great room, still illuminated by a thousand and one candles.*

And now the last guest has been gone for some time, the last huge unwieldy coach has rumbled away, and the dull silence seems to hum and buzz after the clatter of the afternoon and night. He is married. Oliver is still bewildered. He is like one in a dream; he only half knows what he does and says; he only half senses what he sees and hears; his heart thrills almost agonizingly with joy and triumph. Céleste is his, his very own, his wife; and what is more, it has been arranged that he and she are to depart for Flourens — dear, sweet, beautiful Flourens — the very next morning.

Some days before, Oliver had proposed the departure to the marquis, and the marquis had made no objection. He had made but one stipulation, that he himself should remain in Paris.

"There are many matters of business to attend to," he had said. "We have as yet been able to dispose of only a minute portion of our diamonds. The amount we have realized upon them has been enormous, yet it is only a drop or two taken from the bucket."

It had been arranged that Oliver was to see the marquis upon some final business that very night, and so it is that he is now discovered walking so impatiently up and down the empty room at that hour, his heart thrilling with joy and delight. But through all Oliver's joy and delight there ran every now and then a discordant pang of uneasiness, for suddenly, in spite of himself, his thoughts would flash back upon the memory of the master, and under that vivid sinister flash of recollection his soul shrank and trembled within him. Twelve hours still stretched between him and that time of departure. What might not happen in twelve hours?

"Twelve hours," muttered Oliver to himself. "I would give all my diamonds if they were passed and gone." He thought of Céleste, and a keen thrill pierced through his heart; he thought of the master, and another keen thrill—this time heart-sickening—shot through him as the other had done. "No matter," he muttered to himself, "the morning will soon come and we will be miles away, with nothing to fear and with nothing to think of but our love." He pressed his face against the window and looked out into the night, then he turned and pulled out his watch impatiently and looked at it; it was ten minutes of twelve. "I wish he would make haste," he muttered.

As though in answer to his impatient murmur, the door opened and a servant announced that the marquis was ready to see him now in his closet.

Oliver found him seated at his escritoire, with books and papers spread out before him. He took the chair that the marquis indicated, and then the marquis began talking to him. Oliver did not know what he was saying; whenever the other would pause for a reply, he would say, "Yes, yes, that is so," or, "I think not," as the words seemed to demand; sometimes he understood what was said, but more generally it might as well have been spoken in Greek.

"Then," said the marquis, "if I understand correctly, you are entirely satisfied with my management of your affairs?"

Oliver was beginning to grow weary of this business. "Yes," said he, restlessly, "yes, I am entirely satisfied. Manage them as you choose; I do not care; it is of no importance."

The marquis opened his arms. "Embrace me!" he cried. "You are generosity itself; I admire generosity! Your confidence in me touches me. You must know, Oliver, that I manage most discreetly. We have lived here, as you are aware, without stint or economy — it would have been wrong for me to limit that generosity of yours which I so much admire — but yet I have not been extravagant; for not only have we maintained the establishment here in Paris, but we have also paid off the debts upon it, as well as upon Flourens. Yes, Flourens is freed; and I— I am not to be outdone in generosity; those ancestral estates of Flourens that have been in the hands of our family for generations" — he waved his hand — "I give them to you, Oliver, and to Céleste for your own."

"I thank you," said Oliver.

The marquis paused for a moment; his own generosity moved him profoundly. "But I was about to say," continued he, presently, "that the reason more especially why I called you here was to let you see how few of our diamonds have been disposed of. I will show you."

"I do not care to see," said Oliver.

"Pardon me," said the marquis, "but you must see them, my dear Oliver. It is business. Look! yonder is the chest of diamonds. I have had it brought here to-day not only to show you how little of the contents we have as yet disposed of, but also because I expect three merchants from Amsterdam to visit me to-morrow and inspect the gems. They write to me that they have formed a company for the purchase of a quantity of them."

While he was speaking he had taken a bunch of keys from a secret compartment of the escritoire. One of them was the key of the chest. He thrust it into the lock, drew back the bolts, and opened the lid. "You see," said he, "there is not one-tenth of this first tray of diamonds that we have as yet disposed of." Oliver glanced indifferently at them. "The rest of the trays," continued the marquis, "have not yet been touched. I will show them to you."

"I do not care to see them," said Oliver; "I

will take your word for it. If there is nothing further that you care to speak to me about, I would like to be excused; there are many things that I have to prepare for my journey."

"Ah!" said the marquis, "I see these dull affairs of business, they are of no interest to you. Youth is so impetuous! It is better," said he, as he locked the chest and replaced the keys in the secret compartment of his escritoire—"it is better to possess youth and love than all the wealth and gems of the Indies. Go, my dear Oliver, and trust in me. I will manage your affairs, my child, as though they were my own."

Oliver did not wait for a second bidding; he flew from the place and the tiresome talk of diamonds and business. As he was about to enter the room which he had left only a little while before, he hesitated for a moment, he knew not why. A sudden pang shot through him, and he pressed his hand to his bosom. That instant a clock rang out sharply in the silence. He counted the twelve strokes, and then opened the door.

Some one stood looking out of the window, his face close to the glass. He wore a long black cloak, beneath which he carried a large oval frame of some sort. Oliver walked mechanically up the room, and as he advanced that other turned slowly towards him. Oliver's heart gave a great bound, and then stood quite still within him. The next instant every grain of strength seemed to slip away from him; his knees grew suddenly weak and smote together; his hands dropped with a leaden heaviness to his sides, and his tongue clave to the roof of his mouth. *It was the master!*

A moment or two of dead silence followed, and in the heavy, breathless stillness the sharp ticking of a clock sounded with piercing distinctness upon Oliver's tensely-drawn nerves. The master said not a word, but he looked upon him with a cool, contained smile of ineffable complacency.

At last, somehow, Oliver found his voice. "You!" he said, hoarsely; and then again, with a gulp: "You! How came you here?"

The Count de St. Germaine laughed. "How came I here? I walked here. That does not satisfy you? Well, no matter. I have, as you may know, many, very many, ways of coming and going as I choose. Just now it is sufficient that I am here."

"And for what have you come?" said Oliver, in that same slow, hoarse voice.

For a while the master leaned against the deep window-casing, and looked at him from under his brows, his eyes burning like green sparks.

"For what did I come, Oliver?" said he at last. "I will tell you. You must know that I have a silly habit of keeping my promises. Did I not make you the richest man in France? Did I not teach you the secret of the water of wealth? Did I not teach you all that you know, and make you all that you are? Very good. By so doing I fulfilled one part of a promise I some time made you. Now I have come to fulfil the other part. I promised you then that should you ever return to Paris I would ruin you; I am going to ruin you. I promised that I would crush you; I am about to crush you. I promised to make your life a hell; I will make it a hell. I will make you wish a thousand times that you had never been born. When I first met you in Madame de Pompadour's salon, I read in your face your fear that I would betray you. Ah, no! that would have been childish; it would have been petulant; it would have been impatient and premature. No, Oliver; I have waited until now, and what do you think I have waited for?"

Oliver's lips moved, but he could not answer. He stood leaning with his hand upon the side of the table, stunned and dizzied. He felt as though every word that the master spoke struck a leaden blow upon his heart. But the other did not wait for a reply. He flung back his cloak, and brought forth that which he carried beneath it. It was the magic mirror, upon the face of which was drawn the sign that, as Oliver knew, stood between his master and his supernatural power.

The master stood it upon the table beside Oliver, and then, brushing the dust from his hands, turned a smiling face upon his victim.

"You cannot guess?" said he, returning to the question he had asked. "Ah, well, it does not matter. I will tell you. I intend to pierce your heart through that young wife of yours, Oliver."

The words struck upon Oliver's ears like a blow, and like a blow shattered into fragments the dull, heavy, icy despair that rested upon him.

"My wife!" he cried. "My wife! Oh God! You devil! You at least shall die!" His dress-sword hung at his side, and as he spoke he flashed it out.

But the Count de St. Germaine only laughed. "Come," said he, "we are silly; we are childish. Do you think, then, that I am afraid of your sword? Ha!"

As he uttered the exclamation he struck his hands sharply together, and it seemed to Oliver as though the blow had fallen upon him physically. Sparks of fire danced before his eyes; for a few seconds his head spun like a teetotum, and the objects in the room flew around him in a dizzy horizontal whirl. Suddenly the whirling stopped, and as his brain recovered from its confusion, he saw before him again the pale, smiling face of the master. He still held his sword in his hand, but he was powerless. It was as though a leaden weight hung upon his will. He could move neither hand nor foot.

"Put up your sword, my child," said the Count de St. Germaine.

Oliver strove to resist the command, but it was as though his body was not his own—as though the master controlled it. His arm appeared to rise of itself, stiffly, and the sword slid back again into the scabbard.

"Now, then," said the master, "look into the mirror and see what you shall see; it is spoiled forever to my sight, but for you its power is as great as ever. Look!"

Oliver fixed his gaze upon the smooth, brilliant surface of the glass as he was bidden to do. His own face stood there for a moment, then blurred, faded, dissolved. Then on this brilliant surface he saw Céleste.

She stood in her own room as he stood here before the glass—stiffened in every limb—fixed, immovable, as though the same leaden power that overmastered him overmastered her.

The master stood with his eyes fixed upon Oli-

"OLIVER FIXED HIS GAZE UPON THE SMOOTH, BRILLIANT SURFACE OF THE GLASS."

ver's face, and perhaps he saw in that face all that Oliver saw in the mirror.

"Ha!" said he, "it is as I had hoped, my dear Oliver. I congratulate you; your wife is yours in heart and soul. That is the secret of my power over her. I reduce you to my will by my occult power, and at the same time I reduce her also. Observe now what comes of it."

He made a rapid pass in the air, and in an instant Oliver saw Céleste's stiff and rigid form become soft and relaxed. Her face was still white and stony, her eyes were still set intently as ever, but she began moving. Reaching her hand out before her, as though feeling her way in darkness, she passed out of the door of the room.

The master had ceased smiling now, and he stood motionlessly with his gaze fixed upon Oliver's face. His brows were drawn together; his eyes sparkled and glanced like those of a snake; his very head seemed to flatten and broaden like a serpent's when it fixes its victim. He made a quick gesture with his hands, and Oliver saw Céleste stop, take up a cloak from a chair and wind it around her face and body until she was completely disguised. Then she moved again, and presently Oliver saw that she had passed out into the dark court-yard. As she drew near the great gate-way, he saw that it stood open, although, no doubt, the porter had long since closed it. Then, in a moment, Céleste stopped short, and Oliver saw that a coach, with unlighted lamps, stood near at the open gate-way. Suddenly the door of the coach opened, and some one leaped out from within; swiftly, silently, like a hideous distorted shadow. The lanterns at the gate were unlighted, but Oliver knew that distorted, shadow-like figure at once, and as clearly as though he saw it with the eyes of his soul—it was Gaspard. Gaspard thrust his hand into his bosom and drew forth something long and dark. As he approached her Céleste began struggling, as though with the inflexible though invisible power that held her. In her struggles the cloak fell away from her face, and Oliver had one dreadful glimpse of it. The next instant it was hidden. Gaspard, with one sudden movement, and in spite of her blind struggles, had drawn the black bag over her head and shoulders. At that sight Oliver gave a shrill, piping, inarticulate cry. The next instant he saw Gaspard pick her up bodily, and, running forward, fling her limp, death-like form into the coach, leap in himself, close the door with a crash that Oliver almost heard, and the next moment rumble away into the darkness.

"Oh God!" whispered Oliver. "Oh God! Poor Céleste! poor Céleste!"

"That will do," said the master; "you need look no more;" and in answer to his words Oliver turned towards him. A shadow of a dusky pallor lay upon the master's face, and beads of sweat stood on his forehead.

"It is very difficult," he observed, "to psychologize two people at once in this way, and they so far distant from one another. I am glad that Gaspard has taken charge of the case, and removed the strain from me."

Oliver heard the words with a certain dumb consciousness through the agony that hummed in his ears. He felt his face twitching and writhing, and drops of sweat trickled down his forehead. The master replaced his handkerchief and took a pinch of snuff, looking keenly at his victim. "You see," said he, "it is uncomfortable, this being ruined; but then we should have thought of that before we came back to Paris. But I am not yet done with you, Oliver. You have lost your wife; now your wealth must follow. Do you see this?" and he drew something from his pocket and put it upon the table beside him. It was the phial with the black label, marked with this symbol—

that phial which Oliver had brought from the mysterious chambers. "When you and I parted company, Oliver, and I asked you whether you were satisfied with the result of our twelve months of labor, and you said 'Yes,' you did not think of or care for this other bottle; you were contented with the diamonds alone. It would have been wiser, Oliver, if you had insisted upon knowing the properties of this phial of liquor. What they are I will presently show you. In destroying that mirror with your accursed signs you did me irreparable harm. Nevertheless, I know that your diamonds are in this house, for I have, through certain Amsterdam merchants, who are agents of mine, taken care that they should be brought here at this time. Through your present psychological condition, I can also read in your mind that you know where they are. Take this phial, Oliver, and lead the way to them. I will follow, and direct you what further to do."

Once more Oliver strove to resist, but he was powerless. It was as though his will was held in bonds of steel. He took the phial as the master directed, and with the same leaden, heavy steps led the way to the marquis's cabinet, the master following behind him. With the same stiff obedience to the master's will, he went to the escritoire, opened it, brought out the keys, unlocked the chest, and flung back the lid. The master took the bottle from his resistless hand, and uncorked it with his gleaming teeth.

What followed, Oliver only partly saw. He heard a bubbling, hissing sound; he saw a dull, heavy, yellow smoke arise to the ceiling, where it spread out to slowly widening rings. Then it was done, and the master closed the lid.

"And now, Oliver," said he, "since you have been so kind as to do with your diamonds as I desired, I will ask you to do one thing more before we leave this cabinet. Sit down at yonder table, and write a letter. I will dictate it for you."

Again Oliver did as he was bidden; he drew a sheet of paper before him, and dipped the pen into the ink.

"Monseigneur," said the Count de St. Germaine, and Oliver began writing—"I thank you for all of your kindness to me. Those diamonds were false, and more worthless than paste. What they are, you may see for yourself by looking into the chest. I am a charlatan, monseigneur, and have by a trick imposed these artificial diamonds upon you. They have now resolved themselves back into their original form, and I, in the mean time, have escaped from your impending wrath with your daughter, whom I love. It will be useless, monseigneur, for you to seek to discover our hiding-place. Where we have gone you can never follow. Let me say here that my name is not Oliver de Monnière-Croix, but that it is Oliver Munier, and that I am the son of Jean Munier, a poor tailor of Flourens, as you yourself might have discovered had you taken the trouble.

"Adieu, monseigneur, and may better luck attend you at cards than in the choice of your son-in-law. OLIVER."

"There, Oliver," said the Count de St. Germaine, "this letter will, I flatter myself, put the finishing-touch to your ruin. Seal it and address it, and then let us return to the other room. And you shall call the servant and send the letter to papa-in-law."

Once more mechanically obeying, Oliver led the way to the apartment they had quitted. The master pointed to the bell, and in answer Oliver struck it. After some delay the servant appeared, looking with sleepy wonder from Oliver to the visitor, and back again.

Oliver turned to the man, and then he heard his own voice speaking as though it belonged to some one else. "Take this letter directly to your master," said he. "It is of the greatest importance, and bid him from me go instantly to his cabinet. Tell him something has happened to his diamonds, and that he will see it all for himself. Go, I say!"

There was something in his tone, something in his look, that sent the man off like a flash.

The master laughed as the fellow shut the door. "That man," said he, "has never been so surprised in his life before. You should have observed his face when you spoke to him; it was a study. But now I must leave you, Oliver. I have some little matters to attend to, and then I must go and see whether Gaspard has taken your wife to my apartments as I bade him. I am obliged to you for having done everything that I asked you in such an accommodating manner. In return I will give you a piece of advice: go to the river, Oliver, and throw yourself into the water; it is the easiest way to end your troubles. Your wife you shall never see again as long as you live. Your fortune"—he drew his fingers together, and then spread them quickly open with a puff—"it is gone; and papa, the marquis—should you happen to fall into his hands it might be very unpleasant. Yes, take my advice and throw yourself into the water; the disagreeableness will be only for a moment, and then your troubles will be over and done with. Adieu, my child. Now go; it is my order that you drown yourself."

Scene Fourth.—*The marquis's dressing-room.*

The marquis is discovered reclining in dishabille beside a table where some five or six tapers are burning; he has been very wearied with the excitement of the day. But, on the whole, he is satisfied with himself; he is glad that Oliver is going back to Flourens, and still more glad that he will have entire care of the diamonds. He holds a book idly in his hand, and gazes upward at the ceiling as though through a perspective of pleasant inward thoughts. A knock at the door awakens him sharply from his reveries, and the next moment August enters with Oliver's letter.

"What is it?" said the marquis. "Ah! a letter from Oliver, that dear, simple Oliver. Let me see what he has to say." He laid aside his book, and opening the letter, began reading. As he read, the smile faded from his lips, his jaw dropped, his eyes glared, and a heavy, ashy, leaden pallor fell upon his face. As he ended, the letter dropped from his limp hand and fell fluttering to the floor.

Then the marquis rose to his feet; he placed his out-stretched fingers to his forehead, and stood for a moment or two glaring about him. Then the color came flaming back to his face; it grew red, it grew redder, it became purple. Suddenly he roused himself with a choking, inarticulate cry. He snatched up one of the candles from the table and rushed from the room, flinging aside August, who stood in his way, and sent him tumbling backward over a chair and falling with a tremendous clatter to the floor.

He never stopped for an instant until he had reached his private cabinet, into which he burst tumultuously. He tore open the escritoire, and feeling blindly within it, found the key of the chest. Then he dragged forth the chest, and thrust the key into the lock. He flung back the lid, and, leaning over, gazed stupidly down and in.

Where was the glittering treasure that he had left lying upon those velvet-covered trays? It was gone! Nothing left but a mass of muddy charcoal, here and there whitened as though turned to ashes by the touch of fire, and all wet with a pungent fluid that had stained the purple velvet to a dirty reddish-yellow.

"Jean! Edward! François!" It was the marquis's voice, and it rang terribly through the silence of the Hôtel de Flourens.

The next instant there came a crash and a heavy fall, and when the frightened servants crowded around the open door and into the marquis's cabinet, they beheld their master lying upon his face under the table, with an overturned chair upon him, and one arm, with its clinched hand, under his face. He was snoring with stertorous breathing.

"THEY BEHELD THEIR MASTER LYING UPON HIS FACE UNDER THE TABLE."

ACT IV.

Scene First.—*The Seine at midnight.*

Darkness as of death, and, excepting for the hollow murmur of the river, silence as of the grave, utter and profound.

The sky above is a dim, misty opalescence of moonlit stillness; against it rise great, towering, crazy buildings, sharp-roofed, gabled, as black as ink. Across the narrow stretch of intervening water tower other buildings—crazy, sharp-roofed, gabled, as black as ink—and above all loom the great spires of the church into the pale sky, ponderous, massive, silent. One broken strip of moonlight stretches across parapet and roadway of the bridge, white and still. All around it is gaping blackness. Suddenly there is a little movement in the darkness, the sound of a stumbling step, halting and uneven, and then some one appears in the white patch of moonlight. It is Oliver, pale, hollow-eyed, dishevelled, his hair tangled, his lace cravat torn open at the throat, his waistcoat unbuttoned, his silk stockings stained and spattered with mud. He reels like a drunken man as he struggles against the invisible power that holds him relentless as fate. Step by step that power thrusts him, struggling and shuffling, towards the parapet of the bridge. He mounts it and flings one leg over the edge. Beneath him in the inky blackness he can hear but not see the water rushing onward under the arches.

Suddenly some one touched Oliver lightly upon the shoulder, and instantly he felt the same physical effect that had happened when the master had struck his hands together in the room at the Hôtel de Flourens. It was as though a blow had fallen upon him. Bright sparks danced and flashed before his eyes, his brain spun like a teetotum in a dizzy horizontal whirl, and he clutched the cold stones with his fingers to save himself from falling. Then suddenly the sparks vanished and the whirling ceased, and he awoke sharply as though it were from some horrid nightmare. He gazed stupidly around him, still sitting upon the parapet of the bridge; the figure of a woman stood within ten paces of him, her waxy-white face turned full upon him, her unwinking eyes, sparkling in the moonlight, fixed full upon his.

Oliver's heart leaped within him. It was the

"SUDDENLY SOME ONE TOUCHED OLIVER SLIGHTLY UPON THE SHOULDER."

woman whom he had seen in the streets of Flourens that night when the pretended American uncle lodged with him and his mother, and her face looked upon him now just as it had looked upon him when he peered down upon her from the garret window. He slipped from the parapet of the bridge, and, crouching in the shadow on the footway, ran rapidly and noiselessly away from that dreadful, impassive presence. Then, reaching the end of the bridge, and without slacking his speed, he plunged into and wound in and out through the crooked streets, leading he knew not whither. Why he ran he did not know, but something seemed to impel him onward. Suddenly he passed across another patch of moonlight, and as he ran plunging into the shadow upon the farther side, he turned his head and looked over his shoulder. A keen thrill shot through the very marrow of his bones; she was following him—silently, noiselessly, swiftly. He quickened his gait into a run, winding his way in and out through the by-ways. As he passed into and out of the dull red glare of a solitary lantern, he looked over his shoulder again. He could see that dim shape still following him, silent, ghost-like. His heart gave another great leap as it had done at first, and then began to thump against his ribs. The sweat was running down his face in streams, his breath came thick and heavy, and he felt as though he were stifling, but still he ran onward in swift headlong flight, though his feet felt heavy and leaden, as they do in a nightmare dream.

On he dashed through mud and puddles in the crooked streets or on the side-way, for he did not choose his path now through the empty blackness, now across a patch of moonlight, now under the dull glare of a lantern. He had no need to look behind, for his soul knew that she still followed. Suddenly he saw a narrow, crooked passage-way in front of him. Without pausing to think, he doubled like a hare and shot into it. It opened into a stony court surrounded with squalid houses, huge, black, silent. At the farther end was a blind wall, and Oliver's heart crumbled away within him, for an escape was at an end. He darted one look over his shoulder—she was there; he could just see the dim outline of her form flitting through the darkness. The next moment he ran headlong against the wall and there flattened himself, spreading out his palms over the rough surface, hiding his face against his hands, panting and sobbing like a dumb creature.

Five seconds passed, ten, twenty. Oliver looked fearfully over his shoulder, and then hid his face again; she was there, silent, motionless; the faint glimmer of her white face turned full upon him. Again he looked; she neither approached him nor drew away, and by-and-by the impassive harmlessness of her stillness seemed to breathe a breath of softness upon the black rigor of his terror. A faint spark of courage began to glimmer in his heart, and one by one the scattered forces of his will, torn asunder by the tumult of his blind terror, began to gather together and to cohere into some form.

Suddenly there came a quick flash of thought to his mind. It was plain she meant him no harm, and she was in some mysterious way connected with the strange dark life of the master: might she not give him some news of Céleste? He turned suddenly around towards the woman, and instantly as he did so, exactly timing her movements with his, she also turned. Fearing she might escape, he stepped quickly forward; instantly she began to move away; he quickened his pace, she also quickened hers; he began to run, her feet moved quickly, silently; she seemed to make no exertion, but he neither gained nor lost a foot. At last, seeing the uselessness of this crazy race through the silent and deserted streets, he finally stopped; instantly he did so, she also stopped.

"What is it you want of me?" said Oliver. Then, again, receiving no reply, "What is it you want of me?"

Still she made no answer, but stood there motionless, silent.

"Then go your way!" he burst out, desperately, at last. "I know you now. You are like all the rest; you are a devil!"

As he spoke he turned and began to walk away, but he had not gone twenty steps when, looking over his shoulder, he saw that she was following him again, as she had followed him at first. Again he stopped and turned, and again, as though she were his shadow, she also stopped and turned. A long pause of silence followed.

"Madame," said Oliver, at last, "I do not know why you thus choose to dog my footsteps; is there anything that you desire of me?"

No answer.

He waited for a while; the silence weighed upon him like lead. "I have done you no harm," said he, at last; "why do you follow me thus persistently? Are you set as a spy upon me? Surely the master has ruined me enough! Does he desire that I should take my own life? I was about to destroy it when I saw you at the bridge over there."

He waited breathlessly for a reply, but there was no answer.

"Who are you?" he burst out after a while. "You frighten me with your dreadful, mysterious presence! What have I to do with you, or you with me?"

She remained as motionless and as silent as a statue.

"Listen!" said Oliver. "It is less dreadful to follow you than to have you pursue me. Yes, I will follow you. It is but of little consequence whither you take me, for nothing worse can happen to me than that which I have already suffered. Yes, I will follow you." He advanced as he spoke; the woman moved away.

This time Oliver did not hasten his steps as he had done heretofore, but, keeping his eyes upon her, followed her doggedly and stubbornly.

Once more they came out upon the street which they had at first left, and so to the bridge, which they crossed. Now and then, dreading lest he might lose her in the blackness of the night, Oliver hastened his steps, but invariably she quickened hers, so that at last he gave over any fear that she might escape. A hope began to grow and expand in his bosom: whither was she leading him? On and on they went; Oliver took no heed whither. The streets now became broader and better lighted; they had come to a better quarter of the town. But Oliver did not look about him; he kept his eyes fixed upon his mysterious guide; now he did not dare to lose her.

Suddenly she turned at right angles and entered a narrow, closed alley-way. Oliver hurried after, and as he emerged into a little, stony court lit by the dull red glow of a lantern, he saw her whom he followed pause for an instant before a door-way, and the next moment enter.

He leaned against the wall beside which he stood, shuddering and trembling in the rush of a blinding hope. But there was no time for hesitation; he must follow instantly if he would not lose sight of his silent guide. He advanced boldly, and without a moment's hesitation pushed open the door and entered the passage-way within.

SCENE SECOND.—*The master's apartments.*

His guide must have been waiting for him, for, by the light of the lantern without, he saw that silent and mysterious figure moving before him, like a part of the shadowy darkness itself.

For some distance he made his way along the gloomy passage, feeling with his hand against the wall. Suddenly he fell, with a noisy rattle and clatter, upon the lower steps of a stair-way that led steeply up into a yawning blackness above.

He did not hesitate a moment, but began ascending the stairs, still feeling his way with one hand against the wall and the other stretched out in the darkness before him. So he came at last to a little landing-place, and advancing slowly, his other hand presently touched the panels of a door. He fumbled for a second or two until he found the latch, then lifting it with a click, he entered.

The bare, plastered passage-way through which he had come must have been the rear entrance to the apartments above, for, passing through the door, he found himself in what appeared to be a small dining-room, as well as he could see from the light that came from the stair-way beyond. It also seemed to be richly and luxuriously furnished, and he saw the multiple glimmering twinkle of the light in the passage-way beyond flickering upon polished silver and glass.

But he had no time for observation, for before him he saw the figure which he followed just passing through the door upon the other side of the apartment, and he hurried forward without stopping.

Beyond the dining-room he came out upon a broad landing-place of a stair-way, which upon the one hand led to the apartments above, and upon the other to the ground-floor beneath. The flitting, shadow-like figure of his mysterious guide crossed this landing-place to a door-way opposite, and as Oliver, without a moment's hesitation, followed, he found himself in a dressing-room. By the ruddy light of the fire that glowed cheerfully in the grate, he saw that the room was empty; the woman had evidently passed through the door-way upon the other side of the apartment, and so into the room beyond. Again Oliver hurried forward, and laid his hand upon the knob of the door. He tried it; the door was locked.

A hat with a black feather lay upon the table; his eyes fell upon it, and then his heart leaped into his throat. It was the first spark of recognition, and then in a flash that recognition was complete: it was to the Count de St. Germaine's apartments that he had been led by this strange, silent guide.

As Oliver stood there looking about him, a faint sound broke through the stillness—a dull, stifled, moaning cry. Again his heart bounded

"'CÉLESTE!' BREATHED OLIVER THROUGH THE CRACK OF THE DOOR."

within him. He bent his head and listened at the crack of the door. Could he have been mistaken? He fancied that he heard a faint rustling in the room within, and then—yes, there could be no mistake this time! It was the sound of some one crying. "Céleste!" breathed Oliver through the crack of the door.

No answer; even the faint rustling that he had heard had ceased. Oliver's heart throbbed as though it would stifle him; the blood hummed in his ears.

"Céleste!"

"Who is there?" answered a faint voice from within. That voice was sodden and husky with tears, but Oliver recognized it. For a moment or two, in the revulsion of his feelings, he turned giddy and faint. Then he began to cry.

"Oh, Céleste," he sobbed, "it is I—it is Oliver! I am come to save you. Open the door, Céleste, and let me in!"

"I cannot," said Céleste. "It is locked; there is no key."

"But the woman who has just entered," said Oliver, "has she not the key?"

"The woman?" said Céleste. "Of whom do you speak, Oliver? No one has entered here since that dreadful man who brought me here went away and left me."

Oliver looked around him. Could she—that mysterious woman—have left the room by any other way? No; there were but two doors—the door through which he had followed her and the door at which he now stood. She could have left the room in no other way. It was very strange, but Oliver dismissed the subject from his mind. This was no time to wonder over the many mysteries that involved the dark life of the Count de St. Germaine. He must save Céleste. "Courage, Céleste!" he breathed through the door. "I must go and leave you, but I go to bring help to you. I will save you, Céleste!"

He had no plan for saving her, as he thus promised to do; but in the elation of his feelings upon having thus found her, and in the elasticity of his youthful confidence, he felt sure of his ability to do something.

"But, tell me, Oliver," said Céleste, "where am I? Why have I been brought here? What is to happen to me? Who was the horrible man that drew that awful black hood over my face in the garden?"

"You are in the apartments of the Count de St. Germaine," answered Oliver. "He of whom you speak was that Gaspard, and—and I—do not know what they will do to you, Céleste.

But courage, my love. I *must* go; but do not be afraid; I will save you, I swear it! But I must go. If they find me here they will kill me— What was that?"

It was the sound of the closing of a door below; of footsteps crossing the landing upon which Oliver had followed his silent guide.

"Gaspard!"

It was the voice of the Count de St. Germaine!

Oliver stood as though turned to stone.

He cast his despairing eyes around. Where should he escape? To leave by the door was to face the master, whose footsteps he could hear already climbing the stairs towards the room. The window? That meant horrible death upon the pavement beneath.

The wardrobe! The thought was an inspiration. It stood against the farther wall of the room, a huge, ponderous structure of carved and polished wood, inlaid with arabesque patterns of lighter colors. There was no time to lose; the master was almost at the door.

The wardrobe was divided into two compartments separated by a wooden partition, against which the folding doors closed. Oliver climbed into one of the sides and among the clothes that hung from the hooks above, closing the door behind him. As he did so he heard the footsteps of the Count de St. Germaine enter the room.

Gaspard, with his usual silent, cat-like step, must have accompanied the master, bearing a light, for a bright yellow ray fell through the key-hole and traversed the clothes amid which Oliver stood, as though some one crossed the room with a candle.

Oliver scarcely dared breathe as he stood there with palpitating heart, the sweat trickling down his face in streams. He swallowed and swallowed; his mouth was dry and clammy.

The Count de St. Germaine spoke; his voice sounded loud and resonant upon Oliver's tensity of nervous strain.

"Put the lights upon the table there, Gaspard, and bring me my dressing-gown and slippers from the wardrobe yonder."

The words fell upon Oliver's ears like a death-knell. He braced himself to bear the coming shock. It seemed to him that his brain swelled like a soap-bubble, with a hollow, ringing expansion. He heard Gaspard's soft footfalls approaching the closet; it seemed as though it took minutes for him to cross the room. He heard the clever servant's fingers fumbling at the door, and then the wardrobe was opened—but not the side upon which he stood; the dressing-gown and slippers hung in the other compartment.

Oliver's heart gave a great leap, and then he fell to trembling in every joint. Gaspard closed the door of the wardrobe again, and Oliver could hear his soft footfalls recrossing the floor, and then the silky rustling as the master put on the dressing-gown and slippers.

"That is good," said the count. "Now go and bring my chocolate, and then we will look at the girl in the room yonder. She is very pretty."

Oliver heard the words as clearly as though he had been standing beside the speaker. In an instant his prostrating terror vanished like a flash, and in its place blazed up a consuming flame of rage. He clinched his hands together until his finger-nails cut into his palms. He was upon the point of flinging open the door of the wardrobe and bursting out into the room—of clutching that smooth, complacent devil by the throat. Luckily for him, his reason still had some governance over his action. What could he, Oliver Munier, do against the powers of hell that the master had at his command? No; he must wait, he must suffer to the last.

"Yes, monsieur," said Gaspard, and Oliver could almost see the wretch leer.

Then he heard Gaspard close the door. A little time of silence followed. Then the Count de St. Germaine began walking restlessly up and down the room, and after a while he fell to muttering to himself, and as he passed and repassed close by the wardrobe, Oliver could catch snatches of what he was saying.

"What is it that lies upon me to-night? Yes; I feel an influence in this room.—Bah! I am a fool! Why should I fear? I have crushed and annihilated the only one who the stars say could harm me.—Those stars lied. What harm could a heavy, loutish peasant lad do to me?—Yes; he must be drifting down the waters of the Seine by now, rolled over and over, perhaps, in the mud at the bottom.—Peste! To think of his having the wit to destroy that mirror of mine! If I could only consult it now I could make sure that he is out of my way.—Those fools are sometimes possessed with certain cunning of their own." So he continued muttering to himself, passing and repassing the wardrobe.

Presently he stopped in his walk and his soliloquy, and Oliver heard a tinkling chink of china. It was Gaspard bringing in the chocolate. Then he heard the sound of a chair drawn back, and then the faint gurgle of the liquor poured into the cup, the rattle of the sugar in the bowl, and the click of the spoon. There was a pause, and he could distinctly hear the master take a sip. He replaced the cup.

"Now, then, Gaspard, the girl," said he; "bring her—" He stopped abruptly, and a long pause of silence followed. "What!" at length exclaimed the Count de St. Germaine. "Is it you again? What, then, do you desire? This makes the third time this week. Listen! I have warned you, I have besought you, but it seems that I can influence you neither by the one nor the other. I am weary of this importunity. I will reason no more. Gaspard!"

Oliver heard a quick step, a rustling, and then the sound of a fierce, silent struggle. Heretofore he had been afraid to move in the wardrobe; now he could resist no longer. He stooped, and peered through the hole. Just across the room from him was Gaspard, grinning horribly as he struggled silently with some one. Yes; it was with the woman whom Oliver had followed there.

But that struggle lasted only for a moment. The next, Gaspard had drawn his black bag over her head, as Oliver had seen him do once before. Then the struggle instantly ceased, and she stood silent, immovable. Gaspard picked her up, flung her over his shoulder, turned, and the next moment had vanished out of the narrow range of Oliver's outlook, who, however, still remained with his eye glued to the key-hole.

Suddenly an object intervened; it was the back of the master's dressing-gown. Oliver could see nothing but just that little circle of cashmere cloth; the master was not four feet away from him. The cashmere cloth was innocent enough, but the sight of it filled Oliver again with that blind, ungovernable rage. He straightened himself from his observations at the key-hole. But as he did so his elbow struck against the partition alongside of him. He heard a rustle, and knew as well as though he had seen it that his master had turned quickly.

"What is that?" said the Count de St. Germaine's voice, sharply.

Oliver knew that he was discovered, and thereupon his blind rage broke through all restraints of reason and caution. "It is I!" he roared; and flinging wide the door of the wardrobe, he sprang like a cat at the throat of the other. As he sprang he clutched, and as he clutched he felt his fingers instinctively close not only around the soft folds of the cravat, but also around the links of a chain beneath.

The master went staggering back at the unexpected attack, and as he did so his slipper heel

"HE FOUND IN HIS CLINCHED HAND A LACE CRAVAT."

caught in the edge of the rug behind him, and he fell. But as he fell he shouted aloud, "Gaspard! Help!"

It was all over in an instant. The master lay prostrate on the floor, and as Oliver staggered back from the recoil of the attack, he found in his clutched hand a lace cravat and the chain, which had parted from the Count de St. Germaine's neck with a sharp snap. Something hung by the chain. It was a little silver case, thicker than, but about half as long, as a snuff-box.

There was a momentary pause as Oliver stood glaring at the master, still unconsciously clutching the cravat and the chain in his hand. The other had raised himself, and was now staring back at Oliver with wild, dilated eyes, and a face haggard and white as death. The next instant he sprang to his feet.

"My talisman!" he shrieked. "Give it to me!" and he raised his quivering fist in the air as though he would strike Oliver with it.

At the same instant a shrill, exultant voice sounded at the door: "Keep it, Monsieur Oliver, keep it! Do not give it to him! It is his life!"

It was Gaspard who spoke. And as Oliver turned his dazed eyes, he saw the clever servant standing in the door-way, hopping up and down, grinning, wagging his head, and waving his bony, sinewy hands madly hither and thither.

Oliver was stupefied with the tempest of passions that raged in and about him. The master might have taken what he chose, and he could not have moved to resist him. But this the master did not do. He gave a shrill, piping, despairing cry, and the next moment made a rush for the door, his cashmere dressing-gown flying behind him like brilliant wings. He flung Gaspard aside, and the next instant Oliver heard his pattering feet flying up the stairs.

"What does it all mean?" said Oliver, stupidly.

"What does it mean?" cried Gaspard. "Are you a fool? Open the box! open the box!"

Oliver mechanically obeyed him.

Within was a little roll of soft linen, yellow with age. He unrolled it, and within that again found a little crystal ball about the size of a dove's egg. He could see that it contained what appeared to be a dull, phosphorescent mass that, as he held it in his hand, seemed to pulse and throb in the light of the candle; now glowing with a bluish light, now fading away to a dull, milky opalescence.

Again, for the third time, Gaspard's snarling voice broke on his ear. "Oh, thou fool! See him stand like a lump! Pig! Do you not know that the master is busy with his books? A moment more and all is lost! Crush that ball, or you are a dead man!"

His words spurred Oliver to sudden action. He raised the globe high in the air, and flung it upon the floor with all his force. It burst with a flash of light and a report like a pistol, and instantly the air was filled with a pungent, reddish vapor.

The next instant, as the thunder follows the flash of lightning, there came a dull, heavy rumbling, as from the cellar, and the floor swayed beneath Oliver's feet, as though the house were toppling. He looked around; the door-way at which Gaspard had stood was empty; the clever servant was gone.

Then suddenly a confusion of sounds broke upon the stillness of the house: struggles and scuffles, snarling of voices, and squeaking as though of rats, the rattle and crash of furniture pushed about, thumping and banging as of people wrestling and falling against the doors. The next instant there was a sound of a heavy fall, a shrill, long-drawn, quavering scream, and then the lull of dead silence.

Oliver stood like a statue, listening, as though he had been turned to stone. He heard a door open, and then the sound of footsteps, and a strange clacking and clattering upon the stairs without; a heavy panting and breathing. Oliver ran to the door and looked up the stairs. Gaspard was coming down out of the black gloom above. Over his shoulders he carried something limp, like an empty skin or a bundle of clothes tied together. Part of what he carried he dragged clattering down the steps behind him; another part, a round lump the size of a man's head, hung down over his shoulder, wagging from side to side. The next moment the clever servant had come into the square of light from the open door-way of the room. That light fell full upon the round lump that hung wagging from his shoulder, and in the one instant of passing, Oliver saw a dreadful, a hideous face, ashy-white, and with eyes rolled, one upward and one downward, so that only a rim of the pupils showed. The jaws gaped and clapped as the head wagged from side to side. It was the face of the Count de St. Germaine.

Oliver stood spellbound, horrified, watching Gaspard as he descended the steep flight of steps, bearing that ghastly burden. As the clever servant passed under the dull light of the lamp below he turned his head and looked up. His mouth gaped wide with impish, noiseless laughter; he thrust his tongue into his cheek, and

"OVER HIS SHOULDERS HE CARRIED SOMETHING LIMP, LIKE AN EMPTY SKIN, OR A BUNDLE OF CLOTHES TIED TOGETHER."

with an ugly leer and wink of one of his black, bead-like eyes, he passed by and down the steps beyond, the feet of the figure clicking from step to step behind him.

Oliver watched him until he reached the bottom of the steps and passed out from the house into the night beyond; there was the bang of a closing door, and then dead silence.

The next moment Oliver was at the door of the room wherein Céleste was confined. "Céleste!" he screamed, "for God's sake, come! Leave this awful place!"

"What is it?" answered Céleste from within. "Am I then saved?"

"Yes," cried Oliver, in the same shrill voice, "you are saved! But come! come!"

"But the door," said Céleste. "It is locked, Oliver."

"Ah, peste! I had forgotten. Stand away from it." As he spoke, he rushed against the door, flinging himself bodily upon it. It shook, but did not open. Again he dashed himself against it, and this time with better success. The lock snapped, and as it flew open inward Oliver plunged headlong into the room beyond.

Céleste stood, white and terrified, in the middle of the floor. "But am I indeed saved?" said she. "Where, then, is Monsieur de St. Germaine?"

"Do not ask me, Céleste," cried Oliver, hoarsely. "Come!"

As they passed through the room beyond, Céleste looked up into his face.

"What is it?" she cried. "What has happened, Oliver? Tell me."

But Oliver could not answer; he only shook his head.

Upon the landing without, Céleste suddenly stopped and laid her hand upon his arm. "Hark!" said she. "What is that?"

Oliver listened breathlessly. A dull, monotonous sobbing sounded through the house. It came from the apartment above.

"Oh, Oliver!" cried Céleste, "go and see what it is."

Oliver shook his head. "I cannot go," said he, huskily. "I am afraid. You do not know, Céleste, what an awful place this is! If you had seen what I have just beheld—"

"But you must go," said Céleste; "perhaps it is another in trouble like myself. I will wait for you here, Oliver; I am not afraid."

Oliver could not resist such an appeal; he turned, and began heavily ascending the stairs to the floor above. A door at a little distance stood ajar; it was thence that the monotonous sounds came. He advanced hesitatingly towards it, and reaching out his hand, pushed it, and it gaped slowly open upon the room beyond. Oliver only looked within for a moment, and then turned and walked stupidly away, but what he saw in that one glance was impressed upon his mind in an image never to be erased.

Tables and chairs were overturned; books lay torn and scattered upon the floor. In the middle of the room sat the woman whom he had first seen in the moonlit street at Flourens, and her pale, vacant eyes were fixed blankly upon him. Her white lips were slightly parted, but there was never a twitch upon the face that uttered those monotonous sobs that sounded dully through the silence.

Upon the floor lay stretched, bruised, battered, and bleeding, the withered, shrunken figure of an aged man, his limbs a mass of dried skin and bones. The yellow, parchment-like skin was stretched over his head and his face so tightly that it seemed as though it would crack. The shadow of death brooded upon him as he gazed with filmy, sightless eyes into the dark hollow of eternity that lay beyond. His breast, for a long time motionless, now and then heaved convulsively with the laboring breath. Such was the vision that Oliver saw in that one glance. Then he turned and walked away.

"Who was it, Oliver?" said Céleste.

Oliver answered never a word, but taking her by the hand, led her forcibly down the stairs and out of the house.

EPILOGUE.

There was a seven days' gossip in Paris. All manner of rumors were afloat, for strange things had happened at the Hôtel de Flouréns. The marquis had had a sudden stroke of apoplexy upon the very day of his daughter's wedding. But when they had called the family, she and that handsome young husband of hers were nowhere to be found. They had left the hôtel, and did not return again until long after nightfall. Where they had been was a profound secret which they kept locked within their own breasts. But the poor marquis, he was dying. He had never once spoken since he had fallen under the attack. Dr. Raymond-Brasse, and the other physicians who attended him, said that it would be little less than a miracle if he lasted until Wednesday.

Presently other rumors began to get abroad. That vast, fabulous wealth of the interesting Count de Monnière-Croix had vanished; not a crumb of it was left. The debt had been paid off, both upon the château and upon the hôtel, but that was all. It was almost inconceivable that the marquis had squandered that stupendous fortune away in three months, but how else could the matter be explained? It was all very strange and mysterious.

Another thing agitated the world. The Count de St. Germaine had vanished! He had gone! It was rumored that the Prince of Hesse-Cassel had sent for him, and that he had departed. Certainly the Paris world saw him no more.

AFTER THE PLAY.

Ting! a-ling! a-ling! Ring down the curtain, the extravaganza is ended. The red and blue flames are quenched, the pasteboard scenery is pushed back against the wall, the mock jewelry is tumbled into the bandbox, and all the characters have gone into their dressing-rooms to wash the paint off their faces. The lights are out, and nothing is left.

But what does it mean? Who was Monsieur de St. Germaine? Who was Gaspard? Who was the old man who died just now? And that mysterious woman, was she the better life of Nicholas Jovus, which he had materialized along with the evil life? Was it possible that he could not materialize the one without the other? Does it all mean—

"My good friend, why do you ask me? You have seen just as much of this extravaganza as I."

www.ingramcontent.com/pod-product-compliance
Lightning Source LLC
Chambersburg PA
CBHW031942230426
43672CB00010B/2015